Certificate Paper C4

FUNDAMENTALS OF BUSINESS ECONOMICS

For assessments under the 2006 syllabus in 2008

Practice & Revision Kit

In this January 2008 new edition

- Banks of objective test questions on every syllabus area
- Answers with detailed feedback
- Two mock assessments
- Fully up to date as at 1 December 2007

BPP's **i-Pass** product also supports this paper

LEARNING MEDIA

First edition June 2006

Second edition January 2008

ISBN 9870 7517 5183 3 (previous edition 0 7517 2655 9)

British Library Cataloguing-in-Publication Data
A catalogue record for this book
is available from the British Library

Published by

BPP Learning Media Ltd
Aldine House, Aldine Place
London W12 8AW

www.bpp.com/learningmedia

Printed in Great Britain by
Page Bros (Norwich) Ltd
Mile Cross Lane
Norwich
NR6 6SA

We are grateful to the Chartered Institute of
Management Accountants for permission to reproduce
past examination questions. The answers to past
examination questions have been prepared by BPP
Learning Media.

Contents

	Page

Revision

Revising with this Kit iv
Effective revision vi

The assessment

Assessment technique ix
Tackling multiple choice questions xi
Tackling objective test questions xii

Background

Useful formulae and definitions xiv
Useful websites xvi

Question and answer checklist/index xvii

	Questions	Answers

Question practice

Objective test question banks 3 101

Assessment practice

Mock assessment 1 .... 141 159
Mock assessment 2 .... 167 183

Review form & free prize draw

Revising with this Kit

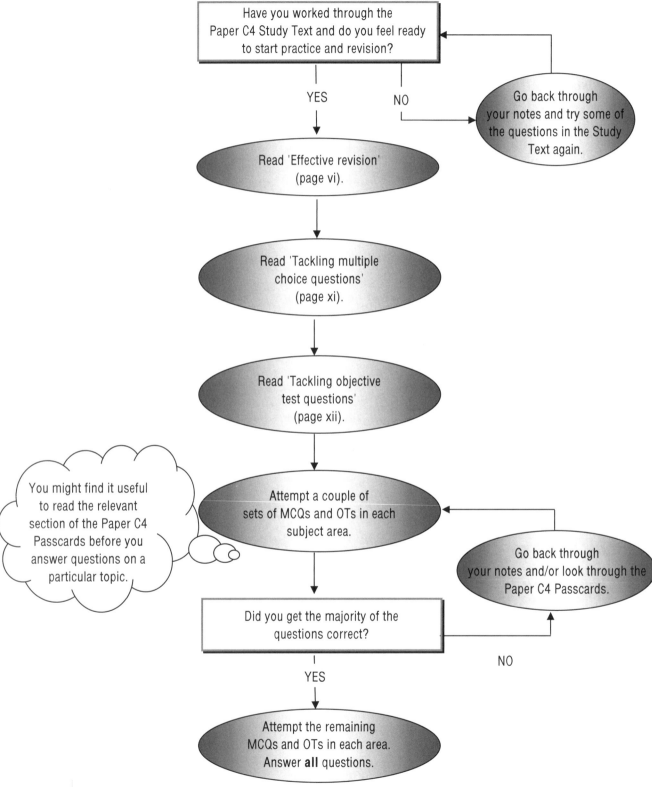

Have you worked through the
Paper C4 Study Text and do you feel ready
to start practice and revision?

YES · NO

Go back through
your notes and try some of
the questions in the Study
Text again.

Read 'Effective revision'
(page vi).

Read 'Tackling multiple
choice questions'
(page xi).

Read 'Tackling objective
test questions'
(page xii).

You might find it useful
to read the relevant
section of the Paper C4
Passcards before you
answer questions on a
particular topic.

Attempt a couple of
sets of MCQs and OTs in each
subject area.

Go back through
your notes and/or look through the
Paper C4 Passcards.

Did you get the majority of the
questions correct?

YES · NO

Attempt the remaining
MCQs and OTs in each area.
Answer **all** questions.

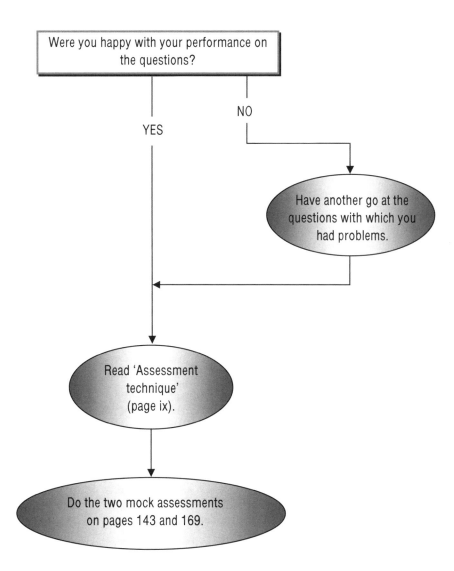

Were you happy with your performance on the questions?

YES

NO

Have another go at the questions with which you had problems.

Read 'Assessment technique' (page ix).

Do the two mock assessments on pages 143 and 169.

Effective revision

This guidance applies if you have been studying for an exam over a period of time. (Some tuition providers are teaching subjects by means of one intensive course that ends with the assessment.)

What you must remember

Time is very important as you approach the assessment. You must remember:

Believe in yourself

Use time sensibly

Believe in yourself

Are you cultivating the right attitude of mind? There is absolutely no reason why you should not pass this **assessment** if you adopt the correct approach.

- **Be confident** – you've passed exams before, you can pass them again
- **Be calm** – plenty of adrenaline but no panicking
- **Be focused** – commit yourself to passing the assessment

Use time sensibly

1 **How much study time do you have?** Remember that you must **eat**, **sleep**, and of course, **relax**.

2 **How will you split that available time between each subject?** A revision timetable, covering what and how you will revise, will help you organise your revision thoroughly.

3 **What is your learning style?** AM/PM? Little and often/long sessions? Evenings/ weekends?

4 **Do you have quality study time?** Unplug the phone. Let everybody know that you're studying and shouldn't be disturbed.

5 **Are you taking regular breaks?** Most people absorb more if they do not attempt to study for long uninterrupted periods of time. A five minute break every hour (to make coffee, watch the news headlines) can make all the difference.

6 **Are you rewarding yourself for your hard work?** Are you leading a **healthy lifestyle?**

What to revise

Key topics

You need to spend **most time** on, and practise **lots of questions** on, topics that are likely to yield plenty of questions in your assessment.

You may also find certain areas of the syllabus difficult.

Difficult areas are

- Areas you find dull or pointless
- Subjects you highlighted as difficult when you studied them
- Topics that gave you problems when you answered questions or reviewed the material

DON'T become depressed about these areas; instead do something about them.

- Build up your knowledge by **quick tests** such as the quick quizzes in your BPP Study Text and the batches of questions in the I-Pass CD ROM.

- Work carefully through **examples** and **questions** in the Text, and refer back to the Text if you struggle with questions in the Kit.

Breadth of revision

Make sure your revision covers all areas of the syllabus. Your assessment will test your knowledge of the whole syllabus.

How to revise

There are four main ways that you can revise a topic area.

Write it!

Writing important points down will help you recall them, particularly if your notes are presented in a way that makes it easy for you to remember them.

Read it!

You should read your notes or BPP Passcards actively, testing yourself by doing quick quizzes or Kit questions while you are reading.

Teach it!

Assessments require you to show your understanding. Teaching what you are learning to another person helps you practise explaining topics that you might be asked to define in your assessment. Teaching someone who will challenge your understanding, someone for example who will be taking the same assessment as you, can be helpful to both of you.

Do it!

Remember that you are revising in order to be able to answer questions in the assessment. Practising questions will help you practise **technique** and **discipline**, which can be crucial in passing or failing assessments.

1   Start your question practice by doing a couple of sets of objective test questions in a subject area. Note down the questions where you went wrong, try to identify why you made mistakes and go back to your Study Text for guidance or practice.

2   The **more questions** you do, the more likely you are to pass the assessment. However if you do run short of time:

  •   Make sure that you have done at least some questions from every section of the syllabus

  •   Look through the banks of questions and do questions on areas that you have found difficult or on which you have made mistakes

3   When you think you can successfully answer questions on the whole syllabus, attempt the **two mock assessments** at the end of the Kit. You will get the most benefit by sitting them under strict assessment conditions, so that you gain experience of the vital assessment processes.

  •   Managing your time
  •   Producing answers

BPP's *Learning to Learn Accountancy* gives further valuable advice on how to approach revision.
BPP has also produced other vital revision aids.

  •   **Passcards** – Provide you with clear topic summaries and assessment tips

  •   **i-Pass CDs** – Offer you tests of knowledge to be completed against the clock

  •   **Success Tapes and Success CDs** – Help you revise on the move

You can purchase these products by completing the order form at the back of this Kit or by visiting www.bpp.com/cima

---

BPP)))
LEARNING MEDIA

Assessment technique

Format of the assessment

The assessment will contain 75 questions to be completed in 2 hours (120 minutes). The questions will be a combination of multiple choice questions and other types of objective test questions.

Passing assessments

Passing assessments is half about having the knowledge, and half about doing yourself full justice in the assessment. You must have the right approach to two things.

> **The day of the assessment**
>
> **Your time in the assessment room**

The day of the assessment

1   Set at least one **alarm** (or get an alarm call) for a morning assessment.

2   Have **something to eat** but beware of eating too much; you may feel sleepy if your system is digesting a large meal.

3   Allow plenty of **time to get to the assessment room**; have your route worked out in advance and listen to news bulletins to check for potential travel problems.

4   **Don't forget** pens and watch. Also make sure you remember **entrance documentation** and **evidence of identity**.

5   Put **new batteries** into your calculator and take a spare set (or a spare calculator).

6   **Avoid discussion** about the assessment with other candidates outside the assessment room.

Your time in the assessment room

1   **Listen carefully to the invigilator's instructions**

Make sure you understand the formalities you have to complete.

2   **Ensure you follow the instructions on the computer screen**

In particular ensure that you select the correct assessment (not every student does!), and that you understand how to work through the assessment and submit your answers.

3 **Keep your eye on the time**

In the assessment you will have to complete 75 questions in 120 minutes. That will mean that you have roughly 1½ minutes on average to answer each question. You will be able to answer some questions instantly, but others will require thinking about. If after a minute or so you have no idea how to tackle the question, leave it and come back to it later.

4 **Label your workings clearly with the question number**

This will help you when you check your answers, or if you come back to a question that you are unsure about.

5 **Deal with problem questions**

There are two ways of dealing with questions where you are unsure of the answer.

(a) **Don't submit an answer.** The computer will tell you before you move to the next question that you have not submitted an answer, and the question will be marked as not done on the list of questions. The risk with this approach is that you run out of time before you do submit an answer.

(b) **Submit an answer**. You can always come back and change the answer before you finish the assessment or the time runs out. You should though make a note of answers that you are unsure about, to ensure that you do revisit them later in the assessment.

6 **Make sure you submit an answer for every question**

When there are ten minutes left to go, concentrate on submitting answers for all the questions that you have not answered up to that point. You won't get penalised for wrong answers so take a guess if you're unsure.

7 **Check your answers**

If you finish the assessment with time to spare, check your answers before you sign out of the assessment. In particular revisit questions that you are unsure about, and check that your answers are in the right format and contain the correct number of words as appropriate.

> BPP Learning Media's *Learning to Learn Accountancy* gives further valuable advice on how to approach the day of the assessment.

Tackling multiple choice questions

The MCQs in your assessment contain a number of possible answers. You have to **choose the option(s) that best answers the question**. The three incorrect options are called distracters. There is a skill in answering MCQs quickly and correctly. By practising MCQs you can develop this skill, giving you a better chance of passing the assessment.

You may wish to follow the approach outlined below, or you may prefer to adapt it.

Step 1   **Note down how long** you should allocate to each MCQ. For this paper you will be answering 75 questions in 120 minutes, so you will be spending on average just over one and a half minutes on each question. Remember however that you will not be expected to spend an equal amount of time on each MCQ; some can be answered instantly but others will take time to work out.

Step 2   **Attempt each question**. Read the question thoroughly.

You may find that you recognise a question when you sit the assessment. Be aware that the detail and/or requirement may be different. If the question seems familiar read the requirement and options carefully – do not assume that it is identical.

Step 3   Read the four options and see if one matches your own answer. Be careful with numerical questions, as the distracters are designed to match answers that incorporate **common errors**. Check that your calculation is correct. Have you followed the requirement exactly? Have you included every stage of a calculation?

Step 4   You may find that none of the options matches your answer.

- **Re-read the question** to ensure that you understand it and are answering the requirement

- **Eliminate any obviously wrong answers**

- **Consider which of the remaining answers** is the **most likely** to be correct and select the option

Step 5   If you are still unsure, **continue to the next question**. Likewise if you are nowhere near working out which option is correct after a couple of minutes, leave the question and come back to it later. Make a note of any questions for which you have submitted answers, but you need to return to later. The computer will list any questions for which you have not submitted answers.

Step 6   **Revisit questions** you are uncertain about. When you come back to a question after a break you often find you are able to answer it correctly straight away. If you are still unsure have a guess. You are not penalised for incorrect answers, so **never leave a question unanswered!**

Tackling objective test questions

What is an objective test question?

An objective test (**OT**) question is made up of some form of **stimulus**, usually a question, and a **requirement** to do something.

- **MCQs.** Read through the information on page (xi) about MCQs and how to tackle them.

- **True or false**. You will be asked if a statement is true or false.

- **Data entry**. This type of OT requires you to provide figures such as the correct figure for GDP in a national income calculation, or words to fill in a blank.

- **Hot spots**. This question format might ask you to identify where on a graph marginal revenue equals marginal cost.

- **Multiple response.** These questions provide you with a number of options and you have to identify those that fulfil certain criteria.

- **Matching.** This OT question format could ask you to classify particular costs into one of a range of cost classifications provided, for example.

OT questions in your assessment

CIMA is currently developing different types of OTs for inclusion in computer-based assessments. The timetable for introduction of new types of OTs is uncertain, and it is also not certain how many questions in your assessment will be MCQs, and how many will be other types of OT. Practising all the different types of OTs that this Kit provides will prepare you well for whatever questions come up in your assessment.

Dealing with OT questions

Again you may wish to follow the approach we suggest, or you may be prepared to adapt it.

Step 1 Work out **how long** you should allocate to each OT. Remember that you will not be expected to spend an equal amount of time on each one; some can be answered instantly but others will take time to work out.

Step 2 **Attempt each question**. Read the question thoroughly, and note in particular what the question says about the **format** of your answer and whether there are any **restrictions** placed on it (for example the number of words you can use).

You may find that you recognise a question when you sit the assessment. Be aware that the detail and/or requirement may be different. If the question seems familiar read the requirement and options carefully – do not assume that it is identical.

Step 3   Read any options you are given and select which ones are appropriate. Check that your calculations are correct. Have you followed the requirement exactly? Have you included every stage of the calculation?

Step 4   You may find that you are unsure of the answer.

- Re-read the question to ensure that you understand it and are answering the requirement
- Eliminate any obviously wrong options if you are given a number of options from which to choose

Step 5   If you are still unsure, **continue to the next question**. Make a note of any questions for which you have submitted answers, but you need to return to later. The computer will list any questions for which you have not submitted answers.

Step 6   Revisit questions you are uncertain about. When you come back to a question after a break you often find you are able to answer it correctly straight away. If you are still unsure have a guess. You are not penalised for incorrect answers, so **never leave a question unanswered!**

Useful formulae and definitions

Set out below are useful formulae and definitions, which you should learn. You will *not* be given these or any other formulae in the exam. You will however, be expected not only to know these but to thoroughly understand the underlying concepts and to be able to apply them. Please note that this list is given for guidance and may not necessarily be exhaustive.

Elasticity of demand

Price elasticity of demand (PED)

(i)   **Point elasticity of demand**

The **point elasticity of demand** measures the responsiveness of demand for a good to a change in its price at a **particular point**, making the assumption that demand is represented by a straight line.

$$\text{PED} = \frac{\% \text{ change in quantity demanded}}{\% \text{ change in price}} = \frac{Q_2 - Q_1}{Q_1} \div \frac{P_2 - P_1}{P_1} = \frac{Q_2 - Q_1}{Q_1} \times \frac{P_1}{P_2 - P_1}$$

where P_1, P_2 = two prices on the demand curve and

Q_1, Q_2 = the two quantities demanded at each of those two price levels

(ii)   **Arc elasticity of demand**

The **arc elasticity of demand** measures the responsiveness of demand between **two points** on the demand curve averaging the price change and the corresponding change in quantity over a **range.**

$$\text{Arc elasticity of demand} = \frac{Q_2 - Q_1}{(Q_1 + Q_2)/2} \div \frac{P_2 - P_1}{(P_1 + P_2)/2} = \frac{Q_2 - Q_1}{Q_1 + Q_2} \times \frac{P_2 + P_1}{P_2 - P_1}$$

where P_1, P_2 = two prices on the demand curve and

Q_1, Q_2 = the quantities demanded at each of those two price levels

Also note the following:

- Since demand falls when the price rises, and vice versa, price elasticity of demand will be a negative amount, although it is usual to ignore the minus sign.

- Note the two extreme values of PED

  Perfectly elastic demand PED = 0

  Perfectly inelastic demand PED = ∞

- Distinguish between elastic and inelastic demand

  Elastic demand PED > 1

  Inelastic demand PED < 1

Cross elasticity of demand (CED)

The cross elasticity of demand measures the responsiveness of demand for one good to changes in the price of another good.

$$CED = \frac{\% \text{ change in quantity demanded of good A}}{\% \text{ change in price of good B}} = \frac{Q_2^A - Q_1^A}{Q_1^A} \div \frac{P_2^B - P_1^B}{P_1^B} = \frac{Q_2^A - Q_1^A}{Q_1^A} \times \frac{P_1^B}{P_2^B - P_1^B}$$

where $\qquad Q_2^A, Q_1^A$ = quantities of product A demanded at price levels P_2^B, P_1^B of product B

When cross elasticity is a *positive value,* goods A and B are substitutes

When cross elasticity is a *negative value,* goods A and B are complements

When cross elasticity is *close to zero,* goods A and B are neither complements nor substitutes.

Income elasticity of demand (IED)

Income elasticity of demand measures the responsiveness of demand to changes in household income.

$$IED = \frac{\% \text{ change in quantity demanded}}{\% \text{ change in income}} = \frac{Q_2 - Q_1}{Q_1} \div \frac{I_2 - I_1}{I_1} = \frac{Q_2 - Q_1}{Q_1} \times \frac{I_1}{I_2 - I_1}$$

where $\quad I_1, I_2$ = two levels of household income

$\qquad Q_1, Q_2$ = the quantities demanded at I_1 and I_2.

Elasticity of supply

Price elasticity of supply (PES)

The price elasticity of supply (PES) measures the responsiveness of supply to a change in price.

$$PES = \frac{\% \text{ change in quantity supplied}}{\% \text{ change in price}} = \frac{Q_2^S - Q_1^S}{Q_1^S} \div \frac{P_2 - P_1}{P_1} = \frac{Q_2^S - Q_1^S}{Q_1^S} \times \frac{P_1}{P_2 - P_1}$$

where Q_1^S, Q_2^S = quantities of product supplied at prices P_1, P_2.

Purchasing power parity theory

The purchasing power parity theory states that changes in exchange rates between two currencies are attributable to the different rates of price inflation in each country.

$$\text{New } e_{F/D} = \text{Old } e_{F/D} \times \frac{1 + P_F}{1 + P_D}$$

where $\qquad$ e = exchange rate denominated as foreign currency/domestic currency

$\qquad P_F$ = Inflation rate in foreign country $\qquad P_D$ = Inflation rate in domestic country

Nominal and real rates of interest

The relationship between the inflation rate, the real rate of interest and the money rate of interest is given by the formula

$$\text{real rate} = \frac{1 + \text{money rate}}{1 + \text{inflation rate}} - 1$$

A good approximation for small values is given by   Real rate = Money rate – inflation rate

Use of computer notation in the computer based assessment

Make sure that you understand and are able to write formulae in computer notation. For example, you can use * on a computer instead of a multiplication sign, or $\land$ if you wish to introduce a power.

Useful websites

The websites below provide additional sources of information of relevance to your studies for *Fundamentals of Business Economics*.

- BPP   www.bpp.com

  For details of other BPP material for your CIMA studies

- CIMA   www.cimaglobal.com

  The official CIMA website

- The Economist   www.economist.com

- Financial Times   www.ft.com

BPP LEARNING MEDIA

Question and Answer checklist/index

	Page number	
	Question	Answer
PART A: The goals and decisions of organisations		
Chapter 1(a): The economic problem	3	101
Chapter 1(b): Economic systems and organisations	7	102
Chapter 2: Theory of costs	11	104
PART B: The market system and the competitive process		
Chapter 3: Price determination – the price mechanism	22	108
Chapter 4: Elasticities of demand and supply	29	111
Chapter 5: Market failures, externalities and intervention	36	115
Chapter 6: Market structures – perfect competition, monopoly, monopolistic competition, oligopoly and duopoly	39	116
Chapter 7: Public policy and competition	54	121
PART C: The financial system		
Chapter 8(a): Finance and financial intermediaries	56	121
Chapter 8(b): Credit and banking	63	123
PART D: The macroeconomic context of business		
Chapter 9: National income accounting	69	125
Chapter 10: Macroeconomic theory	72	126
Chapter 11: Inflation and unemployment	77	129
Chapter 12: Macroeconomic policy	81	130
Chapter 13(a): International trade – the foreign exchange market	85	132
Chapter 13(b): International trade – the international economy	90	134
Mock assessment 1	141	159
Mock assessment 2	167	183

Questions

Chapter 1(a)

The economic problem

This set of questions covers Chapter 1(a) of the BPP Study Text for Paper C4, looking at the economic problem and fundamental economic ideas.

---

1   List the four types of resource known as the factors of production and identify how each is rewarded.

---

2   Fill in the gaps

In a command economy, decisions about resource allocations are made by ....

---

3   Strike out the **words** that are incorrect in the statement below.

Economic costs are also referred to as **opportunity/fiscal/marginal** costs.

---

4   Fill in the gaps.

Normal profit is the opportunity cost of the owner's money and time and the opportunity cost of .... which could have been put to an alternative use.

---

5   Fill in the gap.

The cost of an item measured in terms of the alternatives forgone is called its .... cost.

---

6   A firm making zero economic profit is earning the normal rate of return for the risk undertaken.

☐ True

☐ False

---

7   Fill in the gap.

In a .... economic decisions are made partly by free market forces of supply and demand, and partly by government decisions.

---

8   The basic economic problem facing all economies is:

A   Maximising economic growth
B   Unemployment
C   Inflation
D   Allocating scarce resources

---

9   Opportunity cost is:

    A   The cost of producing one extra unit of the commodity
    B   The lowest average cost of the commodity
    C   The total cost of the commodity
    D   The loss of the next best alternative

10   Which of the following best describes the opportunity cost of a programme of immunisation?

    A   The actuarial valuation of the lives of those who are protected against the disease
    B   The cost of the vaccine
    C   The cost of providing the medical staff
    D   The work the medical staff cannot undertake as a result of the programme

11   In the production possibility diagram below, what combination of X and Y cannot be produced given current levels of resources?

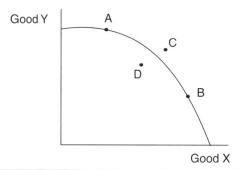

12   Which *one* of the following would *not* shift a country's production possibility frontier outwards (further away from the origin)?

    A   An increase in exports
    B   Technical progress reducing production costs
    C   An increase in the working population
    D   An improvement in the literacy rate

13   Which of the following would *not* be regarded by economists as a factor of production?

    A   Labour
    B   Enterprise
    C   Management
    D   Capital

14 Consider the production possibility curve for the country of Fantasia, shown below. The Fantasian economy is currently operating at point D.

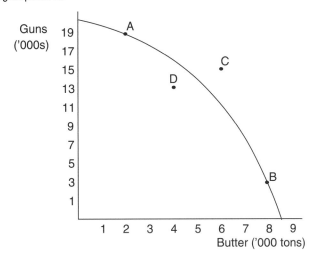

If Fantasia gave up the production of 4,000 guns, how many extra thousand tons of butter could it expect to produce, assuming it used all its resources efficiently?

A   About 2.7
B   About 6.7
C   About 1.5
D   Zero

15 Which of the following will move an economy's production possibility curve (frontier) outwards (away from the origin)?

A   A reduction in unemployment
B   A fall in prices
C   A rise in prices
D   None of the above

16 Which of the following is likely to shift the production possibility curve (frontier) onwards (away from the origin):

A   An increase in specialisation
B   An increase in the labour force
C   An increase in productivity
D   All of the above

17 Which of the following statements about normal profit are correct?

(i)   It is the reward for risk taking
(ii)   It is the return to entrepreneurship
(iii) It is the cost of entrepreneurship
(iv)   It is earned only in the short run

A (i) and (ii) only
B (ii) and (iii) only
C (i), (ii) and (iii)
D (i), (ii) and (iv)

18 In a market economy, decisions and choices about resource allocation are determined by:

A   The government
B   The money markets
C   The price mechanism
D   A combination of market forces of supply and demand, and government decisions

19 The sector of the economy which consists of manufacturing industries is the :

A   Primary sector
B   Secondary sector
C   Tertiary sector
D   Quaternary sector

20 There are four main factors of production, each of which has an economic reward. Which one of the following statements about the factors of production is **not** correct?

A   Capital is rewarded with interest
B   Enterprise is rewarded with profit
C   Labour is rewarded with wages
D   Land is rewarded with property

Chapter 1(b)

Economic systems and organisations

This set of questions covers Chapter 1(b) of the BPP Study Text for Paper C4, looking at the economic goals of, and decisions made by, organisations.

1   The monitoring of the principal-agent problem is the responsibility of

    A   The Government

    B   The Board of Directors

    C   The Financial Services Authority

    D   The Shareholders

2   Fill in the gaps.

    The three types of stakeholder in an organisation are ...., ... and ....

3   Company directors are appointed by:

    A   Auditors

    B   The Board

    C   Senior management

    D   Shareholders

4   The problems associated with the separation of ownership from management and control of a company is referred to as:

    A   The agency or principal-agent problem

    B   The managerial control problem

    C   The efficiency problem

    D   The manager-shareholder problem

5   In a planned economy, the pattern of production is determined by:

    A   Central allocation

    B   Consumer preference

    C   The price mechanism

    D   The profit motive

6   Which of the following is *not* a feature of a mixed economy?

    A   Welfare payments to the long-term sick

    B   Public ownership of all means of production

    C   Government control of interest rates

    D   Private ownership of land

7   An economic system in which both market forces and government planning play a part and in which there is both individual wealth and a government-provided welfare system is called:

    A   A democracy

    B   A mixed economy

    C   A market economy

    D   A common market

8   Is the sum of the cash flows to the contributors of capital to the firm including shareholders and bondholders the free cashflow to *equity* or the free cash flow to the *firm*?

9   Fill in the gap.

    Free cash flows to equity is a measure of what a firm can afford to pay out as ....

10   What does a negative NPV on an investment imply?

    A   The Investment should be undertaken as the future cash flows exceed the cost of the project

    B   The Investment should not be undertaken as the future cash flows do not cover the cost of the project

    C   The Investment should only be undertaken if the firm has no better use for the capital

    D   The firm should take steps to reduce its cost of capital before making future investment decisions.

11   Fill in the gap.

    When using a valuation model to value shares, any increase in the required rate of return will cause the share valuation to.. .

12   Fill in the gap.

    A share valuation will fall as the risks of cash flows ....

13   You have the following information on a company

	$
PBIT	4,000,000
Interest expenses	400,000
Taxes	170,000
Preferred dividends	500,000

    Number of outstanding shares 10,000,000

    Calculate the EPS for this company. [   ]

14   You have the following information on a company

	$
PBIT	4,000,000
Interest expenses	400,000
Taxes	170,000
Capital expenditure	600,000

Calculate the free cash flow to the firm. [   ]

15   You have the following information on a company

	$
PBIT	4,000,000
Interest Expenses	400,000
Taxes	170,000
Capital expenditure	600,000

Calculate the free cash flow to equity. [   ]

16   You have the following information on a company

	$
PBIT	4,000,000
Interest	500,000
PBT	3,500,000
Tax	1,200,000
Profit for year	2,300,000
Assets	50,000,000
Current liabilities	10,000,000

Calculate the return on capital employed (ROCE). [   ]

Consider the following information about a company's results and performance for the year ended 31 December 20X7, then answer questions 17-19 based upon it.

Profit before interest and tax	$29m
Interest charges	$3m
Taxation	$8m
Capital employed	$87m
Number of ordinary shares in issue	15m
Market price of ordinary shares	$6.00

17   What is the company's return on capital employed (ROCE)?

18   What are the Earnings per share?

19 What is the price/earnings (P/E) ratio?

20 Managers have a duty to run their business in a way that best serves the business's purpose. What is this responsibility called?

    A   Autonomous responsibility

    B   Beneficial responsibility

    C   Collective responsibility

    D   Fiduciary responsibility

Chapter 2

Theory of costs

This set of questions covers Chapter 2 of the BPP Study Text for Paper C4, looking at the costs firms incur in producing goods and services, and how they are affected in both the short run and the long run.

1   Fill in the gap.

.... remain constant regardless of the level of production, while .... increase in direct proportion to an increase in output.

2   Match the following

   1   Average Total Costs
   2   Average Fixed Costs
   3   Average Variable Cost
   4   Marginal Cost

   A $\dfrac{\text{Total Cost} - \text{Fixed Cost}}{\text{Total Output}}$

   B $\dfrac{\text{Change in Total Cost}}{\text{Change in Output}}$

   C $\dfrac{\text{Total Fixed Cost}}{\text{Total Output}}$

   D $\dfrac{\text{Total Cost}}{\text{Total Output}}$

3   Match the cost curves on the graph with the correct name below

   I   Average total cost
   II   Marginal cost
   III   Average fixed cost
   IV   Average variable cost

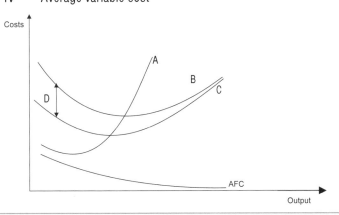

4   The difference between total revenues and total costs (including both implicit and explicit costs) is the firm's:

   A   Accounting profit
   B   Opportunity cost
   C   Opportunity profit
   D   Economic profit

5   Economic costs are

   A   The same as accounting costs
   B   The opportunity costs of the factors of production employed by the firm
   C   Future costs incurred as a consequence of a decision
   D   Explicit costs

6   Accounting profit differs from economic profit as the accounting profit

   A   is based on marginal rather than average costs
   B   ignores depreciation
   C   is based on both implicit and explicit costs
   D   does not take into account the opportunity cost of equity capital

7   A firm has revenue of $2,000,000 explicit costs of $1,200,000 and opportunity costs of equity capital of $120,000 and salary foregone from alternative employment by owner $60,000.

   What is the accounting profit [   ] and economic profit [   ] ?

8   Marginal cost is

   A   The addition to total cost of producing one more unit of output
   B   The total cost dividend by the quantity produced
   C   The total fixed costs and the total variable cost
   D   The difference between fixed and variable cost

9   Average cost is

   A   Variable cost
   B   The cost of producing an additional unit of output
   C   The total of the average fixed cost per unit plus the average variable cost per unit
   D   The minimum manufacturing cost

10 Which of the following statements about economic and accounting profits are correct?

    I   Economic profit of a firm is normally bigger than accounting profit

    II   Accounting profit of a firm is generally bigger than economic profit

    III   Accounting profit is the difference between the firm's revenues and both implicit and explicit costs

    IV   Where the return on the investment is less than the required return for the level of risk undertaken, economic losses are said to be occurring

    A   I and II
    B   II, III and IV
    C   II and IV
    D   IV

11 Fill the gaps

    (a)   When the average total cost is falling, the marginal cost will always be .... than the average total cost

    (b)   When the average total cost is rising the marginal cost will always be .... than the average total cost

12 Which of the following always rise when a manufacturing business increases output?

    I   marginal costs
    II   fixed costs
    III   total costs
    IV   total variable costs

    A   I, III and IV
    B   I and IV
    C   I, II, III and IV
    D   III and IV

13 If a firm's long-run Average Total Cost (ATC) is falling:

    A   There are economies of scale in production
    B   There are diseconomies of scale in production
    C   Costs per unit increase as output increases
    D   Costs per unit remain constant as output increases

14   On the following curve select the correct label for each of the points A, B, C and D with the terms 1-4 below.

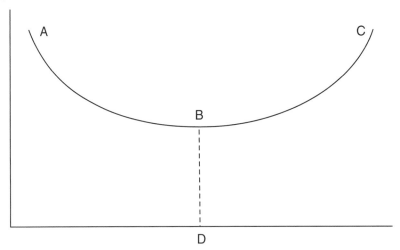

1   Economies of scale
2   Diseconomies of scale
3   Optimal output
4   Constant returns to scale

15   Which of the following would *not* cause cost curves to shift?

A   Technological advances
B   Changes in labour efficiency
C   Changes in demand
D   Increased cost of factors of production

16   It is possible for the average total cost curve to be falling while the average variable cost curve is rising.

☐   True
☐   False

17   Fill in the gap.

Economies of scale that affect a whole industry are called .... economies of scale.

18   Which of the following best describes the law of diminishing returns?

As more labour is added to a fixed amount of capital:

A   Total output will fall
B   Increases in total output will become smaller for each additional unit of labour employed
C   The marginal revenue from each additional unit of output produced will decline
D   Production costs will rise because higher wages will have to be paid to attract more labour

19   The long-run average cost curve for a business will eventually rise because of:

A   The law of diminishing returns
B   Increasing competition in the industry
C   Limits to the size of the market for the good
D   Diseconomies of scale

20   Large firms can benefit from economies of scale, and gain a cost advantage over smaller competitor firms. In spite of this, small firms in industry manage to survive, and there are several reasons for this.

Which of the following is *not* a reason for the survival of the small firm?

A   The minimum efficient scale of production is at a relatively low level of output.
B   Large firms suffer from diminishing returns at higher volumes of output.
C   Small firms are able to fragment the market through product differentiation.
D   Large firms are often bureaucratic and inefficient.

21   Suppose that all inputs are increased by 50%, and as a result, total output increases by 30%.

This would be an illustration of which of the following?

1   The law of diminishing returns
2   Decreasing returns to scale
3   A rising long run average cost curve

A   1 and 2 only
B   2 and 3 only
C   1 and 3 only
D   2 only

22   Which *one* of the following would be a variable cost to a firm?

A   Mortgage payments on the factory
B   The cost of raw materials
C   Depreciation of machines owing to age
D   Interest on debentures

23   Which one of the following statements is incorrect?

A   If the variable cost per unit is constant, a firm would minimise its short-run average cost by producing at maximum capacity.

B   All fixed costs will be incurred in the short run, even if the firm were to shut down.

C   Average variable cost per unit is another expression for marginal cost.

D   When the marginal cost of producing a unit is equal to the marginal revenue from selling it, the firm will make a profit from the unit.

24   ATC = Average total cost
      AVC = Average variable cost
      MC = Marginal cost

      Which of the following statements is correct?

      A   MC will equal ATC when ATC is at its minimum amount, but will not equal AVC when AVC is at its
           minimum.

      B   MC will equal AVC when AVC is at its minimum amount, but will not equal ATC when ATC is at its
           minimum.

      C   MC will equal ATC when ATC is at its minimum amount and AVC when AVC is at its minimum, which
           is at the same output level.

      D   MC will equal ATC when ATC is at its minimum amount and AVC when AVC is at its minimum, but
           this will occur at different output levels.

25   What is the cost label identified as X in the diagram below?

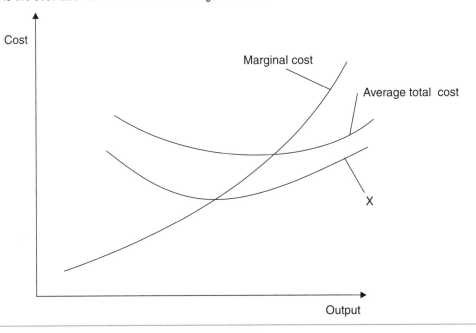

26   Fill in the blank in the sentence below.

      When the average cost curve is falling, the marginal cost curve will be .... it.

BPP
LEARNING MEDIA

27 Between 1970 and 1990 MacDonald's Farm remained the same in size but employed varying numbers of people on the cultivation of grain. The weather was the same each year, but the output varied.

What economic principle is illustrated by the figures given below?

Workers	Output (bushels)
1	270
2	300
3	310
4	314
5	316

....

(write your answer here)

28 Economies of scale cause average cost to decline in the short run.

☐ True
☐ False

29 Which one of the following is *not* a source of economies of scale?

A   The introduction of specialist capital equipment
B   Bulk buying
C   The employment of specialist managers
D   Cost savings resulting from new production techniques

30 Which of the following always rise when a manufacturing business increases its output?

(i)   Fixed costs
(ii)   Marginal cost
(iii)   Average variable cost
(iv)   Total costs

A   (i) and (ii) only
B   (ii) and (iii) only
C   (iii) and (iv) only
D   (iv) only

31 When a firm produces one extra unit of output, what is the marginal cost of the unit?

1   The increase in total cost of production
2   The increase in the variable cost of production
3   The increase in the average cost of production

A   Definition 1 only
B   Definition 2 only
C   Definition 3 only
D   Definitions 1 and 2 only

32   The law of diminishing returns can apply to a business only when:

    A   All factors of production can be varied.
    B   At least one factor of production is fixed.
    C   All factors of production are fixed.
    D   Capital used in production is fixed.

33   Harold Ippoli employs 30 men in his factory which manufactures sweets and puddings. He pays them $5 per hour and they all work maximum hours. To employ one more man he would have to raise the wage rate to $5.50 per man hour. If all other costs remain constant, the marginal cost per hour of labour is now:

    A $20.50
    B $15.00
    C $5.50
    D $0.50

34   A firm operating in a perfectly competitive market will continue production in the short run when

    I   Price exceeds average total cost at the point when marginal revenue equals marginal cost

    II   Price equals average total cost at the point where marginal revenue equals marginal cost

    III   Price is less than average total cost but exceeds average variable cost at the point where marginal revenue equals marginal cost and the price is expected to cover average total cost in the future

    IV   Price is less than average total cost and average variable cost at the point where marginal revenue equals marginal cost although price is expected to cover average total cost in the future

    A   I only
    B   II and III
    C   I, II and III
    D   All of the above

35   Diseconomies of scale occur in a business when:

    A   Minimum efficient scale is reached
    B   Short-run variable costs begin to rise
    C   Diminishing returns to a limited factor of production begin to occur
    D   Long-run average costs begin to rise

36 Which of the following propositions are false?

1 It is possible for the average total cost curve to be falling while the average variable cost curve is rising.

2 It is possible for the average total cost curve to be rising while the average variable cost curve is falling.

3 Marginal fixed costs per unit will fall as output increases.

4 Marginal costs will be equal to marginal variable costs.

A Propositions 1 and 3 are false.
B Propositions 1 and 4 are false.
C Propositions 2 and 3 are false.
D Propositions 2 and 4 are false.

37 Which of the following items could be the cause of diseconomies of scale?

1 A firm has to lower its prices in order to sell a higher volume of output, and so producing more becomes unprofitable.

2 Expansion of the industry as a whole forces up the cost of production resources for firms in the industry.

3 Employees feel a growing sense of alienation and loss of motivation as their firm gets bigger.

A Items 1 and 2 only
B Items 2 and 3 only
C Items 1 and 3 only
D Item 3 only

38 Which of the following statements about the short run marginal cost curve is false?

A Marginal cost equals average cost when average cost is at a minimum
B Marginal cost depends in part upon fixed costs
C When average cost is falling, marginal cost will be below average cost
D Marginal cost will be rising under conditions of diminishing returns

39 Which of the following are true?

I The long run average cost curve shows the minimum average cost of producing at each output level when the firm can choose among all possible plant sizes

II Minimum efficient scale is the point at which long run average costs cease to fall

III The long run average cost curve rises beyond a particular level of output because of diseconomies of scale

A I and II
B II and III
C I and III
D I, II and III

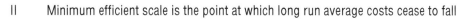

40   Locke and Boult Co is a firm of security guards which provides nightwatchmen to guard the premises of
      client firms. One such firm is Chinese Walls Co, which employs a guard from Locke and Boult for its head
      office building.

      1   The cost of the guard is a variable cost to Locke and Boult, since the number of guards the firm
            employs depends on the demand for their services.

      2   The cost of the guards is a fixed cost to Chinese Walls plc since the employment of the guard is not
            related to the volume of output of the firm.

      3   The cost of the guard is a social cost, since the guard protects the premises of Chinese Walls from
            burglary and fire.

      A   Statements 1 and 2 only are correct
      B   Statements 2 and 3 only are correct
      C   Statements 1 and 3 only are correct
      D   Statements 1, 2 and 3 are correct

41   Muscles Co can only sell more of its product at progressively lower prices. Assuming that there is
      diminishing marginal physical productivity of labour, what implications does this have for the marginal
      revenue product curve (MRP curve) for the firm's labour?

      A   The MRP curve will be completely inelastic.
      B   The MRP curve will equal the average revenue product curve.
      C   The MRP curve will fall faster than if Muscles Co was a perfectly competitive firm.
      D   The MRP curve will no longer be an indicator of wage levels.

42   Decreasing returns to scale only apply:

      A   In the short run
      B   In the long run
      C   If there is one fixed factor of production
      D   If companies have monopoly power

43   The Hoppaboard Bus Company has just replaced its original fleet of four buses, each of which had a crew of
      two, with four new one-man buses. The new buses have the same capacity as the old buses. As a
      consequence, the company has been able to reduce the labour cost per passenger-mile and run the same
      service as before. This is because the company has obtained the benefits of:

      A   Economies of scale
      B   The division of labour
      C   Higher labour productivity
      D   Lower maintenance costs

44 In the short run

A Market participants cannot adjust fully to a change in market conditions
B Producers can alter production levels by expanding the size of their production facilities
C The supply of many goods is relatively elastic
D Both demand and supply are fully flexible

45 When a firm is producing at the lowest point on its average cost curve it is achieving

A Allocative efficiency
B Normal profit
C Equilibrium efficiency
D Technical efficiency

46 A merger between two firms at different stages in the same production process – for example, between an oil extraction company and an oil shipping company – is an example of:

A Horizontal integration
B Vertical integration
C Conglomerate diversification
D Organic growth

47 Chocco makes chocolate bars, and has been successful in recent years. It is looking to grow, through a strategy of horizontal integration.

Which is the most suitable company for Chocco to merge with to achieve this aim?

A Cocoaplant Co, which grows the cocoa used in making the chocolate
B Bitesize Co, a rival manufacturer of chocolate bars
C Dairyway Co, the milk company which supplies the milk for its chocolate
D All Hours Co, a newsagent which sells Choco's products

Chapter 3

Price determination – the price mechanism

This set of questions covers Chapter 3 of the BPP Study Text for Paper C4, looking at the way levels of price and output are determined through the interaction of demand and supply.

1   In a free market economy, the price mechanism:

    A   Aids government control

    B   Allocates resources

    C   Reduces unfair competition

    D   Measures national wealth

2   The supply curve of a firm operating in a competitive market is its

    A   Marginal cost curve above the average variable cost curve

    B   Marginal cost curve above the average total cost curve

    C   Average total cost curve beyond the point where the marginal cost curve cuts it from below

    D   Average variable cost curve below the average revenue curve

3   Giffen goods have an upward sloping demand curve.

    ☐ True

    ☐ False

4   Complete the sentence below.

    If an increase in the price for a good causes an increase in demand for another good, that good is a

    ....

5   Complete the sentence below.

    If an increase in demand for a good causes an increase in demand for another good, that good is a

    ....

6   A rise in household income is likely to result in a leftward shift in demand for inferior goods

    ☐ True

    ☐ False

7   .... is the difference between the price at which a producer would be prepared to sell a good and the prevailing market price.

8   Complements are goods that tend to be bought and used instead of one another.

    ☐ True

    ☐ False

9   Identify from the list below the events that would cause:

A   A leftward shift in the demand curve

B   A righthand shift in the demand curve

Insert A or B

    ☐   1   A rise in household income

    ☐   2   A rise in the price of substitutes

    ☐   3   A rise in the price of complements

    ☐   4   A forecast rise in the price of the good

10   A leftward shift in the *supply* curve will occur if there is a rise in the price of other goods.

    ☐ True

    ☐ False

11   Complete the sentence below.

Some purchasers would be prepared to pay more than the equilibrium price for a good. The extra amount they would be prepared to pay is called ....

12   A legal minimum price is set which is below the equilibrium price. What will be the impact of this?

A   Excess of demand over supply

B   Excess of supply over demand

C   An increase in price

D   Nothing

13   Which one of the following would cause the supply curve for a good to shift to the right (outwards from the origin)?

A   A fall in the price of the good

B   An increase in the demand for the good

C   A fall in production costs of the good

D   The imposition of a minimum price

14   When the price of a good is held above the equilibrium price, the result will be

A   Excess demand

B   A shortage of the good

C   A surplus of the good

D   An increase in demand

15 Which one of the following would *not* lead directly to a shift in the demand curve for overseas holidays?

   A   An advertising campaign by holiday tour operators
   B   A fall in the disposable incomes of consumers
   C   A rise in the price of domestic holidays
   D   A rise in the price of overseas holidays

16 Which of the following is likely to lead to a fall in the price of good Q which is a normal good?

   A   A rise in the price of good P, a substitute for good Q
   B   A fall in the level of household incomes generally
   C   A fall in the price of good T, a complement to good Q
   D   A belief that the price of good Q is likely to double in the next 3 months

17 The demand curve for a product will shift to the left when there is:

   A   A rise in household income
   B   An increase in the product's desirability from the point of view of fashion
   C   A fall in the price of a substitute
   D   A fall in the price of a complement

18 Which of the following is not a substitute for carpet?

   A   Ceramic floor tiles
   B   Wooden floorboard
   C   Vinyl flooring
   D   Carpet underlay

19 Which of the following is not a complement to cars?

   A   Petrol
   B   Tyres
   C   Holidays
   D   Satellite navigation systems

20 The demand for fashion goods is not influenced by:

   A   Price
   B   Allocative inefficiency among producers
   C   The distribution of income among households
   D   Expectation of future price changes

21 Which *one* of the following would normally cause a rightward shift in the demand curve for a product?

   A   A fall in the price of a substitute product
   B   A reduction in direct taxation on incomes
   C   A reduction in price of the product
   D   An increase in the price of a complementary product

22   If the price of coffee falls, which *one* of the following outcomes would be expected to occur?

    A   A fall in the quantity of coffee demanded
    B   A rise in the price of tea
    C   A fall in the demand for drinking cups
    D   A fall in the demand for tea

23   What is an inferior good?

    A   A good of such poor quality that demand for it is very weak
    B   A good of lesser quality than a substitute good, so that the price of the substitute is higher
    C   A good for which the cross elasticity of demand with a substitute product is greater than 1
    D   A good for which demand will fall as household income rises

24   Consider the price and demand for flower vases. The price of cut flowers goes up sharply. Which of the following would you expect to happen?

    A   The demand curve for flower vases will shift to the left and their price will rise
    B   The demand curve for flower vases will shift to the right and their price will rise
    C   There will be a movement along the demand curve for flower vases and their price will go down
    D   The demand curve for flower vases will shift to the left and their price will go down

25   Consider the price and demand for tickets to travel by sea ferry. The price of travelling by hovercraft (a substitute form of travel) goes up. Which of the following would you expect to happen?

    A   The demand curve for sea ferry tickets will shift to the left, and their price will go down. More sea ferry tickets will be sold.

    B   The demand curve for sea ferry tickets will shift to the right, and their price will go up. More ferry tickets will be sold.

    C   The demand curve for sea ferry tickets will shift to the right and their price will go down. More sea ferry tickets will be sold.

    D   The demand curve for sea ferry tickets will shift to the right and their price will go up. Fewer sea ferry tickets will be sold.

26   The summer demand for hotel accommodation in London comes mainly from foreign tourists. Demand for hotel rooms in London in summer could be reduced by a fall in the price or value of which of the following?

    1   US dollars
    2   Aeroplane tickets
    3   Sterling

    A   Item 1 only
    B   Items 1 and 2 only
    C   Items 2 and 3 only
    D   Item 3 only

27 Which of the following changes will cause the demand curve for chocolate to shift to the left?

    1   A fall in the price of chocolate
    2   A health campaign which claims that chocolate makes you fat
    3   A rise in the price of chocolate substitutes
    4   A fall in consumers' income

    A   Change 1 only
    B   Changes 2 and 3 only
    C   Changes 2 and 4 only
    D   Changes 3 and 4 only

28 Suppose that, in a certain advanced industrialised country, the government has applied price controls over rents of both public and private rented accommodation for a number of years, and a serious problem of widespread homelessness has built up. Just recently, the rent price controls have been eased. Which of the following consequences should now occur?

    1   An increase in homelessness
    2   In the longer term, an increase in new building work
    3   The provision of more rented accommodation
    4   Fewer owner-occupied dwellings

    A   Consequences 1 and 2
    B   Consequences 2 and 3
    C   Consequences 3 and 4
    D   Consequences 1 and 4

29 The demand curve for a resource may shift because of

    A   A change in the demand for a good whose production is dependent on the resource
    B   Concerns about potential harmful pollution from the resource
    C   A change in the price of a substitute resource
    D   All of the above

30 The height of the demand curve for a good represents

    A   The minimum price that consumers are prepared to pay for one more unit of the good
    B   The maximum price that consumers are prepared to pay for one more unit of the good
    C   The minimum price needed to cause producers to produce a specified quantity of the good
    D   The opportunity cost of producing the marginal unit of the good

31 All of the following are likely to lead an outward shift in the supply curve for a good, except

    A   The introduction of cost-reducing technology
    B   An increase in the price of the good
    C   A decrease in the price of a resource used to make the good
    D   A decrease in taxes on producers

32   The supply curve for sofas has moved to the right. Which of the following could have caused this shift?

    A   A decrease in the price of sofas

    B   A decrease in the price of futons (a substitute)

    C   A decrease in the cost of horsehair (a raw material used in making sofas)

    D   A decrease in the wage rate in the futon industry

33   When a price floor is imposed above the market equilibrium level

    A   A shortage will result

    B   A surplus will result

    C   Scarcity will result

    D   The good is no longer scarce

34   Consumer surplus is:

    A   The excess between what consumers are prepared to pay for a good or service, and the prevailing market price

    B   The indirect tax producers pay on a good or service

    C   The marginal utility gained by consuming one more unit of a good or service

    D   The indirect tax consumers pay on a good or service

35   In the short run, firms will continue to supply provided that they cover

    A   Fixed costs

    B   Marginal costs

    C   Variable costs

    D   Interest costs

36   Which one of the following would *not* cause a supply curve to shift to the left?

    A   A rise in the cost of factors of production

    B   A rise in household income

    C   A rise in indirect taxes imposed on the good or service being supplied

    D   A rise in the price of other, substitute goods

37   What will happen to a firm's supply curve if government introduces a subsidy for the good the firm produces? ....

38 Indicate whether the following statements would cause a shift in the demand curve, a shift in the supply curve, or neither:

	Shift in demand	Shift in supply	Neither
(i) A change in household incomes			
(ii) A change in the price of raw materials			
(iii) A change in consumer tastes:			
(iv) The imposition of a floor price:			

39 If the demand curve for good A shifts to the *left* when the price of good B rises, what can we say about the relationship between goods A and B?

40 If the demand curve for good A shifts to the *right* when the price of good B rises, what can we say about the relationship between goods A and B?

Chapter 4

Elasticities of demand and supply

This set of questions covers Chapter 4 of the BPP Study Text for Paper C4, looking at the concept of elasticity.

---

1   Annual demand for good A is currently 10 million units at $2.50 each but would be 8 million if they were priced at $3.50 each. Is demand elastic, or inelastic at an output of 10 million units?

---

2   Complete the sentence below.

When demand is elastic, an increase in price will result in a .... in total expenditure.

---

3   The defining characteristic of a Giffen good is that when price increases, demand falls.

☐   True

☐   False

---

4   (i)   What is the formula for calculating cross elasticity of demand?

(ii)   Complete the following sentence.

If the cross elasticity of demand for two goods is positive, the goods are ....

---

5   A supply curve which is a straight line passing through the origin:

A   Is perfectly elastic
B   Has unitary elasticity
C   Is perfectly inelastic
D   Can be either elastic or inelastic

---

6   When price is increased and there is zero change in demand, demand is:

A   Perfectly elastic
B   Unitary
C   Inelastic
D   Perfectly inelastic

---

7   The time horizon is one of the principal factors affecting the elasticity of both supply and demand. Is demand likely to be more or less elastic the longer the timescale?

☐   More

☐   Less

---

8   The elasticity of demand for labour in an industry will reflect the elasticity of the end product.

☐   True
☐   False

9   Which one of the following statements is *not* true?

A   If a good has a price elasticity of demand of 1 at all price levels, total revenue and profit will be the same regardless of the price of the good.

B   When demand is inelastic, an increase in price would cause a fall in quantity demanded, but total revenue from selling the good would rise.

C   When demand is elastic, a fall in price would cause an increase in total quantity demanded so that total revenue from selling the good would rise.

D   A demand curve with a relatively steep slope is usually judged to be inelastic.

10   The demand for a good rises from 20,000 to 25,000 following a reduction in price from $20 to $18.

What is the price elasticity of demand? (using the point elasticity of demand method)

A   −2.1
B   −2.5
C   +2.1
D   +2.5

11   If the demand for a good is *price elastic*, which one of the following is true? When the price of the good:

A   Rises, the quantity demanded falls and total expenditure on the good increases
B   Rises, the quantity demanded falls and total expenditure on the good decreases
C   Falls, the quantity demanded rises and total expenditure on the good decreases
D   Falls, the quantity demanded rises and total expenditure on the good is unchanged

12   Elasticity of demand for labour is influenced by *all* of the factors below except which *one*?

A   The elasticity of supply of alternative factors of production
B   The elasticity of supply of the final product
C   The proportion of labour costs to total costs
D   The ease of substituting other factors of production

13 Which of the following statements is true?

Statement

1   If the price elasticity of demand is more than 1, a fall in price will result in a fall in total expenditure on the product.

2   The income elasticity of demand will only be zero in the case of inferior goods.

3   The cross-elasticity of demand for complementary goods will always be positive.

A   None of them is true.
B   Statement 1 only is true.
C   Statement 2 only is true.
D   Statement 3 only is true.

14 The demand for a product will tend to be inelastic when:

A   It has very few close substitutes
B   It is very quickly consumed
C   It tends to be purchased by people on subsistence incomes
D   It has a wide range of different uses

15 The cross elasticity of demand between widgets and splodgets is 0.6 and the two goods are complements. The price of splodgets goes up by 10%, and demand for splodgets goes down by 15%. Which of the following will happen, in the short run time period?

A   The equilibrium output and price of widgets will *both* fall, but we do not know what either of them will now be

B   The demand for widgets will go down by 6%, and the price of widgets will remain unchanged

C   The demand for widgets will go down by 9%, and the price of widgets will remain unchanged

D   The equilibrium output and price of widgets will change, with price above and quantity demanded below where they were before

16 The demand for a product will tend to be elastic when:

A   It is an essential foodstuff
B   The product is bought mainly by people on subsistence incomes, and accounts for a large part of their disposable income
C   The product has very few close substitutes
D   The product is a cheap, non-durable consumer good that is quickly consumed and takes up only a small part of a household's disposable income

17   If the price elasticity of demand for petrol were zero, what would be the effect of an increase in taxation on petrol?

Effect

1   The consumer would pay all the tax.

2   The quantity of petrol consumed would be unchanged.

3   Total petrol sales would fall (in quantity) by the same proportion as the increase in price caused by the tax.

4   In order to maintain sales volume, petrol stations would have to adopt a pricing policy whereby they absorbed some of the tax.

A   Effect 1 only
B   Effects 1 and 2
C   Effects 2 and 3
D   Effect 4 only

18   A company sells two products, widgets and fidgets. Widgets have a high price elasticity of demand. Fidgets are relatively price inelastic. The company decides to spend $2 million on an advertising campaign for each product, in order to increase demand.

Which of the following statements would be true?

A   The supply curve of both products would shift to the right, and for widgets by a greater proportion than for fidgets.

B   The advertising campaign would be more successful for fidgets than for widgets.

C   The cost of the advertising campaign for fidgets could be covered by raising the price of the product.

D   The supply curve of both products would shift to the left, and for widgets by a greater proportionate amount than for fidgets.

19   A firm's product has a price elasticity of demand equal to unity at all price levels. The current price for the product is P. Which of the following statements is/are correct?

1   Marginal revenue equals zero.
2   Average revenue is constant.
3   Total revenue is at a maximum at the current price level.

A   Statement 1 only is correct
B   Statements 1 and 2 are correct
C   Statements 3 only is correct
D   Statements 1 and 3 are correct

20 The supply of skilled basketweavers is inelastic but not *perfectly* inelastic. There is an improvement in the productivity of basketweavers. Which of the following would you now expect to happen?

A   The number of basketweavers in employment will go down, but their wages will go up
B   The number in employment will be unchanged, and their wages will go up
C   The number in employment will go up, and their wages will go up
D   The number in employment will go up, but their wages will go down

21 When only a small proportion of a consumer's income is spent on a good:

A   The demand for the good will be highly price elastic
B   The good is described as 'inferior'
C   The good is a luxury good
D   The demand for the good will be price inelastic

22 If the demand for a good is price inelastic, which *one* of the following statements is correct?

A   If the price of the good rises, the total revenue earned by the producer increases.
B   If the price of the good rises, the total revenue earned by the producer falls
C   If the price of the good falls, the total revenue earned by the producer increases.
D   If the price of the good falls, the total revenue earned by the producer is unaffected.

23 The price elasticity of demand for a product = 1.
The current selling price per unit is $30.
The marginal cost of producing an extra unit would be $25.
The average cost of production is currently $22.

What would be the effect on total profits of producing and selling one extra unit?

A $5 profit
B $8 profit
C $22 loss
D $25 loss

24 The supply curve of labour will be more elastic:

A   The more training is required for the job
B   The greater the immobility of labour between occupations
C   For a single firm than for the industry as a whole
D   The higher the wage

25   The current price of lawnmowers is P. The supply of lawnmowers is inelastic in the short run, but more elastic in the longer run. The demand for lawnmowers falls. What would you expect to happen?

A   In the short term the price will fall quite sharply, but in the longer term, the price will rise a little as supply is reduced although it will remain less than P.

B   In the short term the price will be unchanged, but in the longer term, the new equilibrium will be at a lower output quantity and a price less than P.

C   In the short term the price will fall quite sharply, but in the longer term supply will be reduced so that the price rises above P.

D   In the short term, the price will be unchanged, but in the longer term the new equilibrium will be at a lower output quantity and a price higher than P.

26   Smudge Paints Co and Dogsbrush Co are leading manufacturers of industrial paints, and their products compete with each other in the market. Which of the following statements would you expect to be correct?

A   The products of Smudge Paints and Dogsbrush have a low positive cross elasticity of demand.
B   The products of Smudge Paints and Dogsbrush have a low negative cross elasticity of demand.
C   The products of Smudge Paints and Dogsbrush have high positive cross elasticity of demand.
D   The products of Smudge Paints and Dogsbrush have a high negative cross elasticity of demand.

27   A demand curve, relating price to output, which is a straight line sloping downwards

A   Has a constant elasticity along its whole length
B   Has a falling elasticity as you move down the line
C   Has a rising elasticity as you move down the line
D   Has an elasticity at each point on the line which has no predictable pattern

28   A burger outlet can sell 20,000 burgers per month at $3 each or 25,000 burgers at $2.60 each. The arc price elasticity of demand is closest to:

A   +1.9
B   +1.6
C   −1.6
D   −1.9

29   On the elastic portion of the demand curve of a good, a decrease in price will lead to which of the following?

	Quantity Demanded	Total Revenue	Marginal Revenue
A	Increase	Decrease	Increase
B	Increase	Increase	Decrease
C	Decrease	Decrease	Increase
D	Decrease	Increase	Decrease

30   The time lag between the decision to increase output and delivery of higher production to the market

   I   is particularly prevalent in primary markets
   II   is referred to as the hog cycle
   III   leads to cyclic variation in supply
   IV   explains the paradox that farmers' incomes tend to vary inversely with levels of production

   A   I and II
   B   I, II, III and IV
   C   II and III
   D   III and IV

31   The implications of delayed supply response to changing prices is referred to as

   A   The cobweb effect
   B   The paradox effect
   C   The cycle effect
   D   The cyclic variation effect

32   Which of the following will lead to an increase in the price elasticity of demand for a good:

   1   A large and increasing number of substitutes
   2   A rise in the proportion of household income spent on the good
   3   A rise in consumer incomes
   4   An increase in the price of complementary goods

   A   1 and 2
   B   1, 2 and 4
   C   2 and 4
   D   2 and 3

Chapter 5

Market failures, externalities and intervention

This set of questions covers Chapter 5 of the BPP Study Text for Paper C4, looking at market imperfections and externalities, and the way government control them through indirect taxes and subsidies.

1   One of the causes of market imperfection is divergence between private costs and social costs.

☐ True

☐ False

2   Complete the sentence below.

When a transaction has an effect that extends beyond the parties to the transaction, that effect is called

....

3   The diagram below illustrates the effect of an indirect tax on the supplier and the consumer of a good. The total amount of the tax is the distance AB. Which part of this is paid by the consumer of the good?

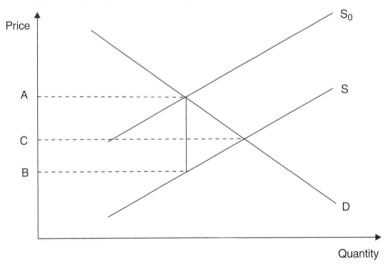

A   AB
B   AC
C   CB
D   None

4   A reduction in government regulation of industry is *unlikely* to produce which of the following undesirable effects?

    A   An increase in market imperfections
    B   Lower quality of service
    C   Cyclical unemployment
    D   Reduced provision of public goods

5   Which of the following are merit goods?

    I   National defence
    II   Health services
    III   Education
    IV   Street lighting

    A   II and III
    B   I, II, and III,
    C   II, III and IV
    D   All of them

6   Muddy Waters Co is an industrial company which has altered its production methods so that it has reduced the amount of waste discharged from its factory into the local river. Which of the following is most likely to be reduced?

    A   Total private costs
    B   Social cost
    C   External benefit
    D   Variable costs

7   Arguments for allocating resources through the market mechanism rather than through government direction include three of the following.

Which *one* is the exception?

    A   It provides a more efficient means of communicating consumer wants to producers.
    B   It ensures a fairer distribution of income.
    C   It gives more incentive to producers to reduce costs.
    D   It encourages companies to respond to consumer demand.

8   The primary burden of a tax will fall most heavily on buyers when

    A   Demand and supply are both elastic
    B   Demand is elastic and supply is inelastic
    C   Demand is inelastic and supply is elastic
    D   Demand and supply are both inelastic

9   The excess burden of tax is minimized when

   A   Demand and supply are both elastic
   B   Demand is elastic and supply is inelastic
   C   Demand is inelastic and supply is elastic
   D   Demand and supply are both inelastic

10   Which of the following solutions to market failure is least likely to distort economic decision?

   A   Establishing property rights
   B   Imposition of a price floor
   C   Imposition of a quota
   D   Subsidy to encourage production

11   Which one of the following is the best example of a public good?

   A   National defence system
   B   Health service
   C   Public transport
   D   Education service

Chapter 6

Market structures – perfect competition, monopoly, monopolistic competition, oligopoly and duopoly

This set of questions covers Chapters 6a & 6b of the BPP Study Text for Paper C4, looking at the output decisions made by firms, and how they vary according to the different market structures in which the firms are operating – perfect competition, monopoly, monopolistic competition, oligopoly and duopoly.

---

1   Fill the gaps

    (a)   If marginal cost is less than marginal revenue then the firm's profits will be .... by making an extra unit.

    (b)   If marginal cost is .... than marginal revenue then the firm's profits will be reduced by making an extra unit.

    (c)   If marginal cost .... marginal revenue, the profit maximising output has been reached and this is the output that a .... firm will decide to supply.

---

2   A perfectly competitive firm will be in equilibrium when price is equal to marginal cost.

    ☐   True
    ☐   False

---

3   An individual firm in long term equilibrium in a perfect competitive market will produce at a level where:

    A   Marginal cost exceeds average revenue
    B   Marginal cost is less than average revenue
    C   Marginal cost and average revenue are equal
    D   Marginal revenue is greater than average revenue

---

4   According to the traditional theory of the firm, the equilibrium position for all firms will be where:

    A   Profits are maximised
    B   Output is maximised
    C   Revenue is maximised
    D   Costs are minimised

---

5   For a profit-maximising firm in conditions of perfect competition, which of the following equations will be true in long run equilibrium?

Equation

1   Average Cost = Average Revenue
2   Marginal Cost = Average Revenue

A   Neither equation is correct
B   Equation 1 only is correct
C   Equation 2 only is correct
D   Equations 1 and 2 are both correct

6

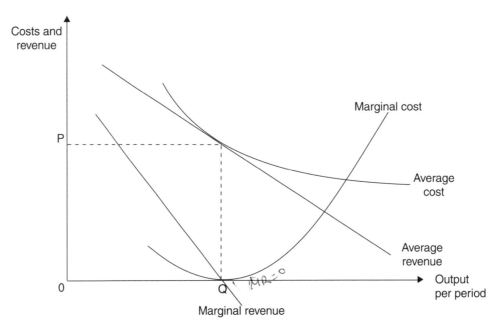

The diagram above shows the cost curves and revenue curves for Hans Tordam Co, a firm of tulip growers. Which of the following statements is true?

Statement

1   Price P and output Q are the profit-maximising price and output levels for the firm.
2   Price P and output Q are price and output levels at which the firm makes normal profits.
3   Price P and output Q are the revenue-maximising price and output levels.

A   Statement 1 only is correct
B   Statements 1 and 2 are correct
C   Statements 2 and 3 are correct
D   Statements 1, 2 and 3 are correct

7   Which of the following statements best describes long run equilibrium in a market where there is monopolistic competition?

A   Marginal revenue equals average cost.
B   There is excess capacity in the industry since firms could reduce average costs by expanding output.
C   Firms will earn supernormal profits because price exceeds marginal cost.
D   Price equals marginal cost, but does not equal average cost.

8   The diagram below shows average revenue and marginal revenue for a price maker? Which is which?

☐   A is marginal revenue, B is average revenue
☐   A is average revenue, B is marginal revenue

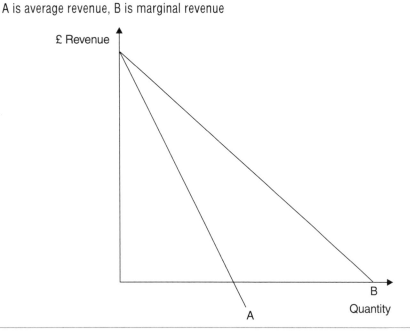

9   Complete the following sentence.

At the output level where marginal cost is equal to marginal revenue, profit is ....

10 The diagram shows a firm operating in a perfectly competitive market. The shaded area ABCD represents:

A Supernormal profit
B Normal profit
C Accounting profit
D Short term loss

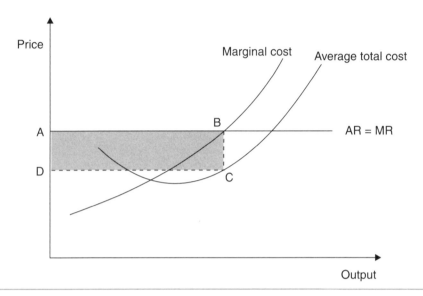

11 The firm operating in a perfectly competitive market attempting to maximize profits should increase output to the point at which

A Average revenue equals average cost
B Average revenue equals marginal cost
C The difference between average revenue and average cost is greatest
D The difference between marginal revenue and marginal cost is greatest

12 The fixed cost of producing garden gnomes is $1. The short run average variable cost of producing a given number of garden gnomes is given below. Also given is the price at which each level of production can be sold.

Output of Gnomes	Short Run Average Variable Cost per Gnome ($)	Price to be Sold at ($)
1	2.20	3.00
2	1.90	2.50
3	1.60	2.10
4	1.53	1.80
5	1.58	1.50
6	1.70	1.20
7	1.87	1.00
8	2.08	0.90
9	2.30	0.80
10	2.55	0.70

What level of output will the profit-maximizing firm choose in the short run?

A   2
B   3
C   4
D   None of the above

13

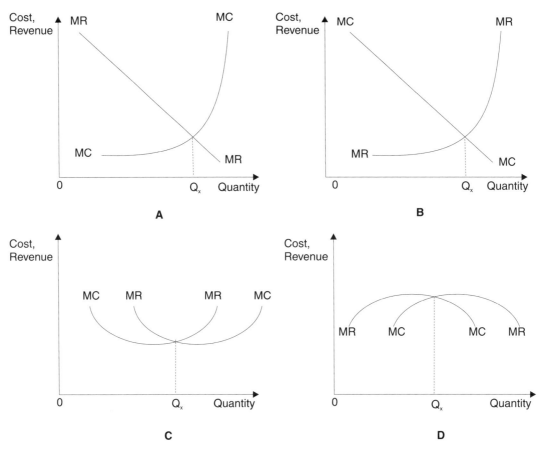

For the given quantity Q_x, which of the diagrams above illustrates a firm maximizing profit?

A   A
B   B
C   C
D   D

14   Complete the following statement.

In conditions of perfect competition, the demand curve for the product of a firm:

A   Is identical to the firm's marginal revenue curve
B   Intersects the firm's marginal revenue curve at the point where MC = MR
C   Is downward sloping
D   Is perfectly inelastic

15   One of the conditions that must apply if perfect competition is to exist is that the products of all the firms in a market must be:

A   Homogenous
B   Heterogeneous
C   Differentiated
D   Unique.

16   Complete the following sentence.

A monopolist will maximise its *sales revenue* when its marginal revenue is equal to

....

17   Elasticity of demand does not affect a monopolist's ability to operate a policy of price discrimination between markets.

✓   ☐   True
     ☐   False

18   A firm operating under conditions of monopolistic competition is a price taker.

☐   True
☐   False

19   What market structure is being described below?

.... differs from perfect competition in that in that there are a small number of firms in the market who will try to avoid competing with each other on the grounds of price.

20   Complete the following sentence.

The kinked demand curve model of oligopoly features a discontinuous .... curve.

21   Monopoly erodes the consumer surplus that would exist under perfect competition. The element of consumer surplus that is totally eliminated is called the:

A   Efficiency loss
B   Deadweight loss
C   Value loss
D   Permanent loss

due to monopoly.

22   Which of the following are characteristics of perfect competition?

    (i)   Large numbers of producers
    (ii)   Differentiated goods
    (iii)   The absence of long-run excess profits
    (iv)   Freedom of entry to and exit from the industry

    A   (i), (ii) and (iii) only
    B   (i), (iii) and (iv) only
    C   (ii), (iii) and (iv) only
    D   All of them

23   Which one of the following is *not* a feature of an industry operating under conditions of monopolistic competition?

    A   There is product differentiation.
    B   Producers operate at below full capacity output.
    C   Firms maximise profits where marginal cost equals marginal revenue.
    D   There is one dominant producer.

24   All of the following are characteristics of a market displaying perfect competition *except* which *one*?

    A   The products are differentiated by advertising.
    B   There are no information gathering costs.
    C   Producers act rationally.
    D   There is a large number of sellers in the market.

25   What is a monopsony?

    A   A market with a single buyer
    B   A market with a single suppliers
    C   A market dominated by a small number of large buyers
    D   A market dominated by a small number of large suppliers

26   Oligopoly markets typically do not display price competition because:

    A   Barriers to entry exist
    B   Products are clearly differentiated
    C   Producers' decisions are interdependent
    D   There is always a price leader

27   A natural monopoly is characterised by:

    A   Being a major part of the primary sector
    B   Technical efficiency
    C   Allocative efficiency
    D   Very high average fixed costs

28   Which of the following arguments could *not* be used to support the existence of monopolies?

    A   Monopolies can achieve maximum economies of scale.

    B   Monopolists can practise price discrimination.

    C   Monopolies can finance more new projects out of retained profits.

    D   Monopoly is efficient in its use of resources.

29   A monopolist's average revenue curve always slopes downwards because:

    A   Economies of scale exist in distribution

    B   There are allocative inefficiencies

    C   Market demand increases as price falls

    D   Marginal revenue can be negative

30   In a perfectly competitive market, all producers charge the same price because:

    A   They are all profit maximisers

    B   They have the same costs

    C   The product is homogeneous

    D   None of the above

31   Which *one* of the following statements is incorrect?

    A   Investment in surplus capacity is a way in which a monopoly firm can try to deter other firms from entering the market.

    B   A natural monopoly is a market in which economies of scale are achievable up to a very high level of output.

    C   Predatory pricing is one method by which firms seek to enter a market which is dominated by a monopoly form or a few oligopolies.

    D   A contestable market is one in which sunk costs are low, so that the costs of entry and exit for predator firms are low.

32   Which *one* of the following statements about price discrimination is incorrect?

    A   Charging a different rate for telephone calls according to the time of day is price discrimination.

    B   Price discrimination might occur for reasons associated with differences in production costs between two or more markets.

    C   Price discrimination between two markets might be achieved because of transportation costs between the markets.

    D   Price discrimination can be achieved by separating markets on the basis of geography, age, time or consumers' ignorance.

33   Which one of the following statements about price discrimination is incorrect?

A   Offering reduced fares on public transport to students would be an example of price discrimination.

B   For price discrimination to be possible, the seller must be able to control the supply of the product.

C   Price discrimination is only profitable where the elasticity of demand is different in at least two of the markets.

D   An example of price discrimination is the sale of first class and second class tickets on an aeroplane journey.

34   The conditions necessary for a successful policy of price discrimination by a company include which of the following?

(i)   There are at least two separate markets
(ii)   Marginal costs are different in each market
(iii) The price elasticities of demand are different in each market
(iv)   The price elasticities of demand are the same in each market

A   (i) and (ii) only
B   (i) and (iii) only
C   (i), (ii) and (iii) only
D   (ii) and (iv) only

35   Which *one* of the following will tend to increase competition within an industry?

A   Economies of scale
B   Barriers to entry
C   Low fixed costs
D   Limited consumer knowledge

36   Which *one* of the following would *not* act as a barrier to the entry of new firms into an industry?

A   Perfect consumer knowledge
B   Economies of scale
C   High fixed costs of production
D   Brand loyalty

37   The purpose of a cartel is to:

A   Rationalise production
B   Reduce consumer uncertainty
C   Standardise product quality
D   Ensure that a dominant group of producers all charge the same price

38   A firm that is technically efficient is one which:

A   Uses up-to-date machinery

B   Produces a given quantity of output with minimum quantity of inputs

C   Produces a given quantity of output such that the price of the output equal the marginal cost of production

D   Substitutes machinery in place of labour to improve output quantities

39   Which of the following statements about the behaviour of a profit-maximizing monopoly is true?

A   It will only produce at the level of output where the price elasticity of demand is greater than one

B   It will only produce at the level of output where price is equal to marginal cost

C   It will set a price less than marginal cost but greater than average cost

D   It will set a price where marginal cost is at a minimum

40   Monopolies maintain supernormal profits in the long run because

A   They are more efficient than other firms

B   Unlike other firms, they benefit from economies of scale

C   They can advertise

D   There are barriers to the entry of competitors

41   Which one of the following does not constitute a barrier to entry into a monopoly market?

A   Significant economies of scale

B   Constant long run average costs

C   Heavy advertising costs

D   Large-scale capital requirements

42

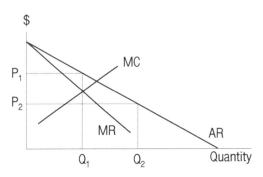

The diagram above shows a profit-maximizing monopoly producer of high-definition television sets that was originally producing at Q_1 with price P_1 and marginal cost curve MC and marginal revenue curve MR. Now, as a result of changed conditions (not shown), it sets a price P_2.

This change could have occurred because of

A   An increase in consumer incomes

B   A reduction in labour costs

C   An increase in research costs

D   A fall in the price of normal television sets

43   Which of the following statements about the conditions necessary to achieve the specified outcomes is correct?

A   Firms wishing to maximise their profits should increase output until marginal revenue exceeds marginal costs

B   Monopolies wishing to maximise sales revenue should produce an output such that the price elasticity of demand is equal to zero

C   Competitive firms aiming to maximise sales revenue should set price equal to marginal cost

D   Firms wishing to minimise costs should produce such that marginal costs equal average costs

44   If five firms each have a market share of 18% and the remaining 10% of the market is shared among 20 small firms, the resulting market structure is

A   Monopoly

B   Oligopoly

C   Monopolistic competition

D   Perfect competition

45 Collusion in oligopolistic markets will lead to

A Firms setting price where industry marginal revenue is equal to marginal costs and supernormal profits being earned

B Firms setting price where industry marginal revenue is equal to marginal costs, and normal profits being earned

C Firms setting price equal to average total cost, and supernormal profits being earned

D Firms setting price equal to average total cost, and normal profits being earned

46 Price discrimination in monopoly markets can be used to

A Increase output and allocative inefficiency
B Increase output and reduce allocative inefficiency
C Reduce output and allocative inefficiency
D Reduce output and increase allocative inefficiency

47 Which of the following would you expect to be the long run attributes of an industry under monopolistic competition?

I Firms operate below full capacity
II Each firm faces a horizontal demand curve
III There is product differentiation

A I and III
B II and III
C II and I
D None of the above

48 The Herfindahl index measures

A Market concentration
B Distribution of income
C Profit levels
D Sales trends

49 The leading companies in an industry have sales as follows.

Co	A	B	C	D	E	F	G	H
Sales ($m)	10	15	17	19	26	14	18	20

Total industry sales are $143m.

What is the five firm concentration ratio for the industry?

A   61%
B   68%
C   70%
D   75%

50 A Herfindahl index of zero indicates

A   Oligopoly
B   Pure monopoly
C   No merger and acquisition activity
D   Perfect competition

51 Complete this statement.

.... is characterised by a large number of producers making extensive use of product differentiation. .... is characterised by interdependence of decision making on price and output between firms.

A   Perfect competition: oligopoly
B   Perfect competition: monopolistic competition
C   Monopolistic competition: oligopoly
D   Monopolistic competition: perfect competition

52 What theory can be used to illustrate how competition between firms in an oligopoly or a duopoly can lead to inefficiency, because resources are used without generating corresponding benefits?

....theory.

53 CM Co operates in a perfectly competitive market. The best way for the firm to increase its profits is to

A   Raise prices
B   Reduce costs
C   Set barriers to entry
D   Increase production

54   In an industry with no barriers of entry and with ease of both exit and entry

    A   Oligopolies will prevail
    B   Monopoly will prevail
    C   Higher than normal economic profits will appear in the long run
    D   Higher than normal economic profits will be eliminated in the long run

55   Total *revenue* for a firm with a downward sloping demand curve will be maximised when

    A   Marginal cost = marginal revenue
    B   Marginal cost = average revenue
    B   Average cost = average revenue
    D   Marginal revenue is zero

56   Which of the following may be barriers to entry preventing new firms from entering an industry?

    I   High fixed costs
    II   Patents
    III   Branding
    IV   Perfect knowledge

    A   I and II
    B   II and III
    C   I, II and III
    D   All of them

57   What are the missing phrases?

A major difference between monopolistic competition and oligopoly is that oligopolistic markets have
.... which enable .... to be maintained in the long run.

    A   Product differentiation; supernormal profits
    B   Product differentiation; normal profits
    C   Barriers to entry; supernormal profits
    D   Barriers to entry; normal profits.

58   It is not always necessary to have many firms supplying a market for conditions similar to perfect competition to apply. If entry and/or exit from a market is easy such that the number of firms could change depending on the levels of profit earned, firms will face a market structure similar to the perfect competition model, even though there may currently only be a few firms in the market.

What type of market is being described here?

    A   Concentrated market
    B   Contestable market
    C   Convertible market
    D   Consumer market

Chapter 7

1   Regulatory capture occurs when:

    A   An indirect tax is imposed on imports

    B   Government imposes rationing during a crisis

    C   A regulator closes a loop hole

    D   Regulators act in the producers' interests rather than consumers'

2   How many of the following are arguments in favour of privatisation

    (i)   Privatised companies may be more efficient than nationalised companies

    (ii)   Denationalisation will create wider share ownership, which will encourage staff to develop a better understanding of their business and profit drivers

    (iii)   Privatised companies may have a more profit-oriented management culture than nationalised ones

    (iv)   Industries can benefit from significant economies of scale arising from natural monopolies

    A   1

    B   2

    C   3

    D   4

3   In the UK, who would the Director General of Fair Trading ask to investigate the market if any firm or group of firms controlled more than 25% of that market?

    A   Office of Fair Trading

    B   Competition Commission

    C   European Commission

    D   Secretary of State

4   Which of the following is *not* an argument in favour of privatisation?

    A   Privatisation provides a source of money for the government

    B   Privatisation reduces bureaucracy and political meddling in the industries concerned

    C   Privatised industries are more likely to respond to the public interest

    D   Privatisation encourages a more profit-oriented management culture

5   Fill in the gap.

The ....enlists private sector capital and management expertise to provide public services at reduced cost to the public sector budget in the UK.

A   Public Accounts committee
B   Private Finance Initiative
C   Competition Commission
D   Office of Fair Trading

Chapter 8(a)

Finance and financial intermediaries

This set of questions covers Chapter 8(a) of the BPP Study Text for Paper C4, looking at the flow of funds in an economy and the role of financial intermediaries.

---

1   Venture capital is best described as:

   A   Investment funds provided for established companies
   B   Short-term investment in eurocurrency markets
   C   Capital funds that are highly mobile between financial centres
   D   Equity finance in high-risk enterprises

---

2   When a financial intermediary (such as a building society) provides short-term facilities for savers and long-term ones for borrowers, they are performing:

   A   Maturity transformation
   B   Risk transformation
   C   Liquidity transformation
   D   Interest transformation

---

3   A financial intermediary is best defined as:

   A   An institution that matches lenders' supply of funds with borrowers' demand for funds

   B   An institution that operates on the Stock Exchange, matching buyers and sellers of stocks and shares

   C   An institution that allows firms to obtain equipment from suppliers by providing leasing or hire purchase finance

   D   An institution that acts as a buffer between the Bank of England and the rest of the UK banking system (*Discount House*)

---

4   Maturity transformation is:

   A   The process by which loans get closer to redemption as time passes
   B   The amount payable to redeem a loan or security at its maturity
   C   The way in which interest rates vary according to the duration of the loan
   D   The process by which short term deposits are re-lent by banks as longer term loans

---

5   Which *one* of the following is *not* a part of the equity capital market?

   A   Pension funds
   B   Retail banks (*take deposits → later → loans*)
   C   Life assurance companies
   D   Venture capital organisations

6　Which of the following is *not* a source of finance for households?

A　Bank overdraft
B　Credit cards
C　Commercial Paper
D　Hire Purchase

7　Which of the following are *not* negotiable instruments?

(i)　Bank overdraft
(ii)　Bill of exchange
(iii)　Commercial paper
(iv)　Certificate of deposit

A　(i) only
B　(i) and (ii)
C　(ii) and (iii)
D　(i), (ii) and (iv)

8　Which of the following is *not* a method a firm can use to finance its long-term investments?

A　Retained profits
B　Bank overdraft
C　Bank loan
D　Issue of new shares

9　Which of the following is the most suitable source of finance for a company undertaking a major long-term investment project?

A　Bank overdraft
B　Five year bank loan
C　Bill of exchange
D　Share issue

10　Financial intermediaries

A　Decrease the level of liquidity in the economy
B　Reduce risk through diversification
C　Are unable to bring together borrowers and lenders
D　None of the above

11　Financial intermediaries borrow funds from ultimate lenders and lend it to ultimate borrowers.

☐　True
☐　False

QUESTIONS

12   Fill in the gaps.

.... is concerned with risks that might occur: .... is concerned
with risks that will occur.

13   Direct finance in the flow of funds scheme:

A   Takes place without the use of a financial intermediary
B   Takes place through financial markets
C   Normally involves governments and companies
D   All of the above

14   Indirect finance in the flow of funds scheme:

A   Involves the use of a financial intermediary
B   Involves the transfer of only large amounts of money from one unit to another
C   Is used by corporations only
D   All of the above

15   Which of the following is not a type of financial intermediary?

A   Pension funds
B   Banks
C   Insurance companies
D   Households

16   The interbank market is the market in which .... lend .... funds to one another.

A   Banks, long-term
B   Insurance Companies, Long-term
C   Bank, short-term
D   Insurance Companies, Short-term

17   Financial instruments with maturities of less than one year are traded in the

A   Equity market
B   Capital market
C   Money market
D   Fixed-income market

18   A 30-year Treasury bond that was issued in last year is sold in a:

    I   money market
    II   capital market
    III   primary market
    IV   secondary market

    A   Both I and III.
    B   Both I and IV.
    C   Both II and III.
    D   Both II and IV.

19   Markets for newly issued financial instruments with maturities shorter than one year are

    I   money markets
    II   capital markets
    III   primary markets
    IV   secondary markets

    A   Both I and III.
    B   Both I and IV.
    C   Both II and III.
    D   Both II and IV.

20   Which of the following is a money market instrument?

    A   A treasury bill
    B   A government bond
    C   A corporate bond
    D   A mortgage loan

21   Which of the following is a capital market instrument?

    A   A certificate of deposit
    B   A bill of exchange
√   C   Commercial paper
    D   Preference share

22   Suppose that you have the choice of two investments carrying similar levels of risk, one is short term and the other is a long term bond. Would you expect the interest on the longer term bond to be

    A   Normally higher
    B   Lower
    C   Normally the same
    D   Impossible to tell

23   If the market rate of interest rises, the price of bonds will:

A   Rise
B   Stay the same
C   Fall
D   Fluctuate both up and down

24   The bond equivalent yield of a Treasury Bill is based on 360 day calendar

☐ True
☐ False

25   A primary market is a market for newly issued securities

☐ True
☐ False

26   Which of the following is a government obligation?

A   Gilts
B   Commercial paper
C   Preference shares
D   Ordinary shares

27   The main difference between government bonds and corporate bonds is

A   The coupon they pay
B   Their face value
C   Their maturity
D   Their risk

28   A.......................................bond allows the issuer to redeem the bond earlier than its maturity date.

A   Convertible
B   Callable
C   Zero coupon
D   Perpetual

29   A.......................................bond allows the conversion of.......................................into shares

A   Callable, money market instruments
B   Convertible, bonds
C   Callable, bonds
D   Perpetual, bonds

30   ...., have priority over..

A   Preference shares, Bonds
B   Preference shares, Ordinary shares
C   Ordinary shares, Preference shares
D   Ordinary shares, Bonds

31   In..preference shares if a firm does not distribute dividends in any year, these unpaid dividends are carried forward from year to year.

A   Redeemable
B   Participating
C   Cumulative
D   Convertible

32   Which of the following is a major reason for the existence of financial intermediaries?

A   The existence of long-term financial instruments
B   Problems related to asymmetric information
C   The inability to borrow funds directly from savers
D   The need to avoid government regulation in other financial markets

33   Which of the following requires financial intermediaries?

A   Direct finance
B   Indirect finance
C   Direct purchase of retail goods
D   None of the above

34   .... and .... normally pay a fixed amount per year

A   Preference shares, Bonds
B   Ordinary shares, Bonds
C   Preference shares, Treasury bills
D   Ordinary shares, Treasury bills

35   The process by which an insurer spreads risks with another insurer in exchange for part of the premiums is:

A   Broking
B   Underwriting
C   Reinsurance
D   Affiliation

36   Which of the following financial intermediaries specialize in making mortgage loans?

A   Pension funds
B   Building societies
C   Finance companies
D   Insurance companies

37   What is the role of insurance companies?

A   To provide liquidity
B   To transform the maturity of assets
C   To transfer risk
D   To provide an investment vehicle

38   In a whole life policy the length of the contact is:

A   Fixed
B   Variable
C   Flexible
D   Indefinite

49   In a term life policy the length of the contact is:

A   Fixed
B   Variable
C   Flexible
D   Indefinite

40   Which of the following market participants are not involved in the secondary markets?

A   Traders
B   Underwriters
C   Brokers
D   Pension fund managers

41   Which of the following statements is not true?

A   A bond can be traded in the primary market
B   A bond usually has a fixed maturity
C   A corporate bond holder is entitled to a share of the profits of the company
D   A bond pays a fixed coupon

42   Which of the following is *not* a function of money?

A   A store of value
B   A unit of account
C   A certificate of deposit
D   A medium of exchange

Chapter 8(b)

Credit and banking

This set of questions covers Chapter 8(b) of the BPP Study Text for Paper C4, looking at the role of banks and financial markets in the economy

1   Which *one* of the following is *not* a function of a central bank?

A   The conduct of fiscal policy
B   Management of the national debt
C   Holder of the foreign exchange reserves
D   Lender of the last resort

2   Which *one* of the following would appear as a liability in a clearing bank's balance sheet?

A   Advances to customers
B   Money at call and short notice
C   Customers' deposit accounts
D   Discounted bills

3   Which of the following is a liquid asset, that is, one that may readily be converted into cash without loss of face value?

A   Government stock
B   Shares in a bank
C   Fine art paintings
D   Money market deposits

4   Which one of the following is *not* likely to increase the rate of interest a business borrower has to pay on a loan?

A   An extended period of credit
B   Low financial gearing
C   A project based on specially developed technology
D   A low level of physical assets

5   Which *one* of the following is *least* likely to influence the rate of interest a business is charged on a loan?

A   Existing levels of debt of the business
B   The rate of corporate tax paid by the business
C   The business's past trading record
D   The availability of assets to secure borrowings

6   Which *one* of the following would you expect to be included in 'broad money' but *not* in narrow money?

    A   Banks' till money
    B   Clearing banks' operational deposits with the central bank
    C   Banks' retail deposits
    D   Bank notes in circulation

7   The credit multiplier is the process by which:

    A   An injection of government spending increases national income
    B   The relationship between the value of a bank's deposits and its cash holdings is governed
    C   Cash leaks out of the banking system into less formal accumulations
    D   Government controls the creation of credit

8   What are the three main aims of a commercial bank which it must try to keep in balance?

    A   Profitability, liquidity, security
    B   Profitability, credit security
    C   Prudence, liquidity, savings
    D   Prudence, credit, savings

9   Which of the following is a central bank least likely to be responsible for?

    A   Fixing the general level of interest rates
    B   Regulating the banking industry
    C   Determining the public sector borrowing requirement
    D   Maintaining national reserves of foreign currency

10   Which *one* of the following is *not* fundamental to retail banking operations?

    A   Profitability
    B   Liquidity
    C   Security
    D   Elasticity

11   The central bank influences interest rates by:

    A   Controlling the amount of notes and coins in circulation
    B   Changing the reserve requirements
    C   Setting the rate at which it lends funds to commercial banks
    D   Imposing credit limits

12   Which of the following are normally functions of a central bank?

(i)   Issuing notes and coins
(ii)   Supervision of the banking system
(iii)   Conducting fiscal policy on behalf of the government
(iv)   Holding foreign exchange reserves

A   (i), (ii) and (iii) only
B   (i), (ii) and (iv) only
C   (i), (iii) and (iv) only
D   (ii), (iii) and (iv) only

13   Which of the following items will *not* be found in the assets of a retail bank?

A   Overdrafts
B   Bank bills
C   Customers' deposits
D   Loans to the money markets

14   A banking system in a small country consists of just five banks. Each bank has decided to maintain a minimum cash ratio of 10%. Each bank now receives additional cash deposits of $1 million. There will now be a further *increase* in total bank deposits up to a maximum of:

A $500,000
B $5 million
C $45 million
D $50 million

$$C + A = \frac{C}{r}$$

$$D = \frac{C}{r} = \frac{1}{0.40} = 10$$

$$D \times 5 = 50 \qquad D = C + A = 5\!\!\!- \quad A = 50 - 5$$
$$= 45$$

15   If all the commercial banks in a national economy operated on a cash reserve ratio of 20%, how much cash would have to be deposited with the banks for the money supply to increase by $300 million?

A $60 million
B $75 million
C $225 million
D $240 million

$$C + 300 = \frac{C}{0.2}$$

$$C + 300 = \frac{10C}{2}$$

$$2C + 600 = 10C$$

$$\frac{300}{4} = \frac{600}{8} = C$$

$$\overset{\shortmid}{=} 75$$

16   One of the largest assets on banks' balance sheets is customers' deposits

☐ True
☐ False

17   A bank keeps on hand as reserves all of the money entrusted to its deposits

☐ True
☐ False

.he following statements is true?

fhe potential deposit expansion multiplier is 1 minus the required reserve ratio

The actual deposit expansion multiplier will be reduced if individuals hold currency rather than depositing it in a bank.

The actual deposit expansion multiplier will be increased if individuals hold currency rather than depositing it in a bank.

D   The actual deposit expansion multiplier is the multiple by which an increase in reserves will decrease the supply of money.

19   When a central bank purchases government securities, this will tend to:

I   Reduce the monetary base
II   Reduce the money supply
III   Increase the money supply
IV   Increase the monetary base

A   I and III only
B   II and IV only
C   II and III only
D   III and IV only

20   If expected inflation is negative, the nominal interest rate is..than the real interest rate, and..

A   Greater, positive
B   Greater, negative
C   Less, positive
D   Less, negative

21   For which of the following is the current yield the most accurate representation of the true yield on the bond?

A   Treasury bill
B   A five-year bond
C   A ten-year bond
D   A thirty-year bond

22   The running yield of a bond is defined as

A   The ratio of coupon to the face value of the bond
B   The ratio of coupon to the market value of the bond
C   The coupon plus the capital gain from the bond
D   The return from the bond when held to maturity

23   The redemption yield shows the return from investing in a bond which is held until maturity.

☐   True
☐   False

24   The yield curve shows the relationship between bond yields of various maturities.

☐   True
☐   False

25   Suppose that you have bought 1000 shares at a cost of $6 per share. You receive 3c per share in dividends, and sell the shares in a year's time at $6.50 per share. What is rate of return on your investment?

✓   A   1%
     B   8.33%
     C   8.83%
     D   9.33%

$$Ke = \frac{d}{P} + g = \left(0.03 + \frac{(6.50 - 6)}{6}\right)$$

26   The yield from an investment is

A   The redemption value of a bond
B   The coupon payable on a bond
C   The short-term interest rate
D   The measure of the return on an investment

27   If interest rates go up, the required rate of return on equities will go...and equity prices will...

     A   Up, rise
✓   B   Up, fall
     C   Down, rise
     D   Down, fall

28   A bond has a nominal value of $1,000, and a nominal interest rate of 4%.

If the current market price of the bond is $800 what is the current yield on the bond?

A   3.2%
B   4%
C   5%
D   6.4%

$$y_c = \frac{C}{P} = \frac{40}{800} = 0.05 = 5\% \quad ✓$$
$$y_N = \frac{C}{F} \Rightarrow C = y_N \times F = 0.04 \times 10^3 = 40$$

29   If the cash reserve ratio (or reserve asset ratio) is 20%, what will be the total amount of money created from an initial deposit of $100?

$$R = \frac{D}{r} = \frac{100}{0.2} = 500$$

A $200
B $300
C $400
D $500

30   If the nominal rate of interest in Erewhon is 15% per annum and the annual rate of inflation is 6%, what is the real rate of interest?

A   8%

B   8.5%

C   8.7%

D   9%

$$\frac{1+0,15}{1+0,06} = 1+r$$

$$r = 8,50$$

Chapter 9

National income accounting

This set of questions covers Chapter 9 of the BPP Study Text for Paper C4, looking at how we measure the level of economic activity in a country.

1   Label the diagram below using the list of terms provided.

Factor incomes

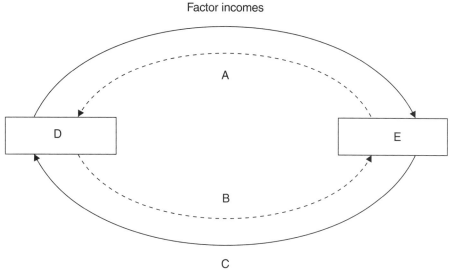

A

D

E

B

C

1   Firms
2   Households
3   Factors of production
4   Goods and services
5   Expenditure on purchases

2   What are the withdrawals from the circular flow of income in the economy?

3   Insert the missing term in the equation below.

GDP + ... = GNP

4   Insert the missing term in the equation below.

National income = GNP – ....

5   GNP (Gross National Product) at factor cost may be best defined as:

    A   The total of goods and services produced within an economy over a given period of time.

    B   The total expenditure of consumers on domestically produced goods and services.

    C   All incomes received by residents in a country in return for factor services provided domestically and abroad.

    D   The value of total output produced domestically plus net property income from abroad, minus capital consumption.

6   If there is a reduction in government spending, there will not necessarily be a fall in National Income if there is an increase in:

    1   Exports
    2   Taxation
    3   Investment

    A   1 and/or 2
    B   1 and/or 3
    C   2 and/or 3
    D   Any of 1, 2 and 3

7   Net National Product at factor cost
    + Capital consumption
    + Indirect taxes on expenditure
    – Subsidies
    equals

    A   Gross National Product at market prices
    B   Gross National Product at factor cost
    C   Gross Domestic Product at market prices
    D   Gross Domestic Product at factor cost

8   Which of the following cannot be termed a 'transfer payment' for the purpose of National Income accounting?

    A   Interest paid to holders of government stock
    B   Salaries paid to Members of Parliament
    C   Payments of state pensions
    D   Social security payments

9   Which of the following investments creates an injection into the circular flow of income?

    A   An increase by a firm in its inventories of finished goods, prior to a marketing campaign

    B   The purchase by a pension fund of shares in a newly privatised company

    C   The purchase of a second-hand piece of farming machinery with their savings by a farming co-operative group

    D   The takeover of one company by another company

10 The following data relate to National Income statistics in Muvovia, which are compiled in the same way as in the UK.

	20X6 Actual prices $ million	20X7 Actual prices $ million
Consumers' expenditure	200,000	225,000
General government final consumption	70,000	74,000
Gross domestic fixed capital formation	54,000	60,000
Imports	92,000	99,000
Exports	93,000	94,000
Taxes on expenditure	52,000	50,000
Subsidies	8,000	10,000

The general rate of inflation in Muvovia between 20X6 and 20X7 was 10%. The *real* change in Gross Domestic Product at market prices between 20X6 and 20X7, in percentage terms, was:

A   A fall of about 1%

B   A rise of about 1%

C   A rise of about 5%

D   A rise of about 9%

11 Which *one* of the following statements is correct?

A   Two countries with the same total National Income will have roughly the same living standards.

B   Services provided free to the public, such as police work and state education, are valued at opportunity cost in the National Income statistics.

C   Official statistics might over-estimate the National Income for a country with a strong black economy.

D   Gross National Product figures are often used in preference to Net National Product figures because of the difficulty in calculating capital consumption.

12 A country has a GDP at factor cost of $150m.

Government expenditure was $25m, subsidies were $10m and taxes were $17m.

What is its GDP at market prices?

A $143m

B $157m

C $168m

D $182m

Chapter 10

Macroeconomic theory

This set of questions covers Chapter 10 of the BPP Study Text for Paper C4, looking at the way aggregate demand and aggregate supply combine to determine the level of national income.

1   Identify the full employment level of real national income on the diagram below.

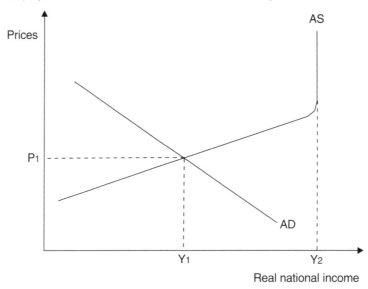

☐ P$_1$
☐ Y$_1$
☐ Y$_2$

2   On the diagram below, what does the distance P_1P_2 represent?

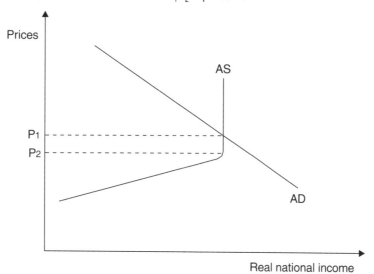

Prices

AS

P_1

P_2

AD

Real national income

A   Inflationary gap
B   Deflationary gap
C   Unemployment
D   Nominal interest rate

3   Fill in the gaps.

A redistribution of income from rich to poor households is likely to lead to .... in aggregate demand because the poorer households have a higher ....

A   An increase; marginal propensity to save
B   A decrease; marginal propensity to save
C   An increase; marginal propensity to consume
D   A decrease; marginal propensity to consume

4   In Dumnonia, the marginal propensity to consume is 0.9. The Dumnonian government injects $2bn into the economy. What is the theoretical increase in national income that should ensue?

5   The accelerator principle explains how capital investment changes in direct proportion to changes in consumption.

☐   True
☐   False

6   The marginal propensity to consume measures

A   The relationship between changes in consumption and changes in consumer utility
B   The proportion of household incomes spent on consumer goods
C   The proportion of total national income spent on consumer goods
D   The relationship between changes in income and changes in consumption

ccelerator principle states:

How an initial increase in a component of national income leads to much greater eventual rise in national income

B   That a small change in investment will lead to a much greater change in the output of consumer goods

C   That a small change in the output of consumer goods will lead to a much greater change in the production of capital goods

D   That changes in investment level are the cause of trade cycles

8   Which of the following can indicate trade cycle movements?

Item

1   Raw material prices
2   Gross Domestic Product
3   Seasonal unemployment

A   Items 1 and 2 only
B   Items 2 and 3 only
C   Items 1 and 3 only
D   Items 1, 2 and 3

9   The effect of the multiplier on national income will be small:

A   When there is high unemployment in the economy
B   When the marginal propensity to save is low
C   Because of a deflationary gap
D   Because of leakages from the circular flow in addition to savings

10   Which of the following is the correct sequence in a business cycle?

A   Boom, Recession, Depression, Recovery
B   Recession, Recovery, Boom, Depression
C   Boom, Recovery, Recession, Depression
D   Recovery, Recession, Depression, Boom

11   Other things remaining the same, according to Keynes, an increase in the money supply will tend to reduce:

A   Interest rates
B   Liquidity preference
C   The volume of bank overdrafts
D   Prices and incomes

12   The Keynesian view of inflation is associated with *which* of the following concepts?

    A   Rational expectations of inflation

✓ B   Supply side economics   ✓

    C   The natural rate of unemployment

    D   The inflationary gap

---

13   The multiplier principle explains how investment in capital goods responds disproportionately to changes in consumer demand.

☐ True

☐ False

---

14   In Fitzrovia, the marginal propensity to consume is 0.8. The Fitzrovian government injects $2bn into the economy. What is the theoretical increase in national income that should ensue? ☐

---

15   Keynes argued that an increase in the money supply would lead to .... interest rates while monetarists argue that an increase in the money supply would lead to .... inflation.

    A   Lower; lower

✓ B   Lower; higher

    C   Higher; lower

    D   Higher; higher

---

16   An equal rise in government purchases and taxes raises output.

✓ ☐ True

   ☐ False

---

17   The recession phase of the trade cycle will normally be accompanied by all of the following *except* which *one*? ↓inflation

    A   A rise in the rate of inflation →

    B   A fall in the level of national output   ✓

    C   An improvement in the trade balance → ↓imports

    D   A rise in the level of unemployment

---

18   All of the following will normally cause a fall in the level of economic activity in an economy *except* which *one*?

    A   A rise in cyclical unemployment   ✓

    B   A fall in business investment

    C   A decrease in government expenditure

    D   A rise in interest rates

19   If the marginal propensity to consume in an economy is 0.6, what is the marginal propensity to save in that economy?

    A   0.4
    B   0.6
    C   1.6
    D   Will depend on the level of national income

20   In Gondwana, an open economy, for every additional $1 of income, 20% is taken as taxes, 10% is saved and 50% is spent on domestically produced goods. What is the value of the multiplier in Gondwana?

    A   0.8
    B   1.25
    C   2
    D   3.33

21   An economy which does not participate in international trade, and whose government does not make injections or withdrawals into the circular flow has a full employment level of $200m. The current level of national income is $175m.

Assuming that the marginal propensity to consume is 0.8, how much additional investment is needed in order to reach the full employment level of national income?

    A $5m
    B $10m
    C $20m
    D $25m

Chapter 11

Inflation and unemployment

This set of questions covers Chapter 11 of the BPP Study Text for Paper C4, looking at two of the key aspects of macroeconomics – inflation and unemployment.

1   The diagram below shows how a price shock can lead to stagflation. Has the aggregate supply curve moved from left to right or from right to left?

☐ Left to right
☐ Right to left

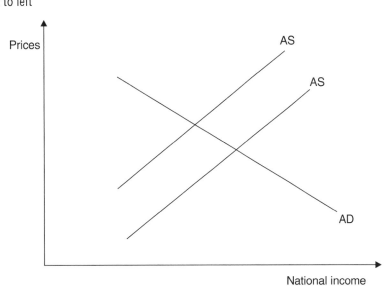

2   If the real rate of interest is 3% pa and the expected rate of inflation is 6% pa, the nominal interest rate will be approximately:

A   ½%
B   2%
C   3%
D   9%

3   A government may seek to reduce the rate of demand-pull inflation by any of the following means *except*:

A   Reducing interest rates
B   Increasing value added tax
C   Applying more stringent controls over bank lending
D   Reducing public expenditure

4   A county's consumer price index changed from 100 to 120 over a period of twelve months to December 2007 and national income also rose from 600 to 690 for the same period.

What is the adjusted 2007 national income, after adjusting for inflation?

A   525
B   575
C   620
D   670

---

5   Structural unemployment is best defined as unemployment caused by:

A   Defects in the industrial and commercial structure
B   A long-term decline in a particular industry
C   A mismatch between available jobs and the unemployed
D   A switch from labour-intensive to capital-intensive production methods

---

6   Imports are a source of cost push inflation.

☐   True
☐   False

---

7   Complete the sentence below.

Unemployment caused by long-term changes in the conditions under which an industry operates is called

.... unemployment.

---

8   Unemployment that rises and falls in a regular pattern not associated with the overall economic cycle is called .... unemployment.

A   Cyclical
B   Frictional
C   Seasonal
D   Residual

---

9   Complete the sentence below.

.... unemployment is best tackled by supply side measures. Demand management can only affect .... unemployment.

A   Structural; frictional
B   Frictional; cyclical
C   Structural; cyclical
D   Cyclical; structural

10 Label the axes of the diagram of the Phillips curve below in the boxes provided.

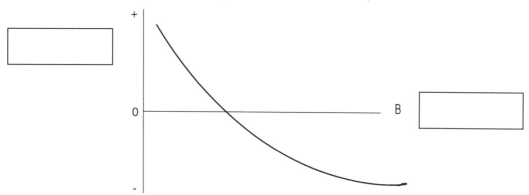

11 What is the five-letter acronym used to denote the unemployment rate associated with the long-run Phillips curve?

....

12 Complete this sentence.

A .... represents the extent to which the planned level of aggregate demand will need to shift upwards to reach the full employment level of national income.

13 Inflation caused by a persistent excess of aggregate demand over aggregate supply is called demand push inflation.

☐ True
☐ False

14 Which of the following would *not* lead to cost push inflation?

A   Rising import prices

B   Increase in wages

C   Increases in indirect taxation

D   High consumer expenditure such that aggregate demand exceeds aggregate supply

15 Unemployment that occurs in specific industries as a result of long-term changes in the patterns of demand and supply is:

A   Seasonal
B   Structural
C   Cyclical
D   Frictional

16   The .... says that the expansion of aggregate demand to reduce unemployment below its natural rate will only produce inflation.

A   Short-run Phillips curve
B   Natural rate hypothesis
C   Equilibrium rate hypothesis
D   Wage control hypothesis

17   Which *one* of the following measures has *not* been recommended by Friedman and the monetarist economists as a means of reducing the natural rate of unemployment to a lower level?

A   Measures to stimulate consumer demand for more goods
B   Schemes to retrain workers in new job skills
C   Measures to cut trade union power
D   Restructuring the income tax system

18   All of the following measure might be used by a government to help to control cost-push inflation *except*:

A   A revaluation/appreciation of the currency
B   Higher direct taxation
C   Measures to control 'wage drift'
D   Linking public sector pay increases to productivity improvements

19   Which *one* of the following measures would be expected to reduce the level of unemployment?

A   An increase in value added tax
B   A higher budget surplus
C   A reduction in employers' National Insurance contributions
D   A reduction in investment in the nationalised industries

Chapter 12

Macroeconomic policy

This set of questions covers Chapter 12 of the BPP Study Text for Paper C4, looking at the way macroeconomic goals are achieved through fiscal and monetary policy.

1   Which of the following is not part of government purchases of goods and services?

   A   Salaries of public servants
   B   Repairs of public buildings
   C   Investment in infrastructure
   D   Unemployment and welfare payments

2   The budget deficit is defined as:

   A   The gap between government expenditure and government receipts
   B   The gap between government expenditure and tax receipts
   C   The gap between government purchases and tax revenues
   D   The net interest paid on outstanding debt

3   A budget deficit.. government debt.

   A   increases
   B   decreases
   C   has no effect on
   D   eliminates

4   The government debt represents:

   A   The gap between government purchases and tax revenues
   B   The amount of outstanding gilts the government has issued
   C   The total government expenditure of the government
   D   All of the above

5   For the Quantity Theory of Money equation (MV = PT) to explain short-run price behaviour, it is necessary that:

   A   P varies inversely with M
   B   Interest rates remain unchanged
   C   Changes in V in the short run are predictable
   D   The number of transactions remains unchanged

6   Using the new quantity theory of money identity MV ≡ PQ, if the velocity of circulation and level of national output remain constant but the money supply grows by 5%, what will happen to inflation?

   Increase/Decrease by ☐ %

7   Which of the following should result from a government policy of high interest rates? (Tick all that apply.)

    A   ☐   Lower consumer demand
    B   ☐   Less overseas investment in the currency concerned
    C   ☐   Slower growth in the money supply

8   Which of the following are effects of reduced interest rates?

    (i)   Consumer spending will increase
    (ii)   Business investment will be encouraged
    (iii)   Saving will increase

    A   (i) only
    B   (i) and (ii)
    C   (ii) and (iii)
    D   All of them

9   A cut in interest rates will result in higher private spending and a higher equilibrium output.

    ☐   True
    ☐   False

10 The government of a certain country decides to introduce a new tax, which will involve a flat charge of $200 on every adult member of the population. This new tax could be described as:

    A   Regressive
    B   Proportional
    C   Progressive
    D   Ad valorem

11 If a reduction in the taxes on alcoholic drinks resulted in a less even distribution of wealth in society, with a greater proportion of wealth in the hands of the rich sections of society, we could conclude that, *on average*:

    A   People with low incomes spend more on alcoholic drinks than people with high incomes

    B   People with low incomes spend less on alcoholic drinks than people with high incomes

    C   People with low incomes spend a bigger proportion of their income on alcoholic drinks than people with high incomes

    D   People with low incomes spend a lower proportion of their income on alcoholic drinks than people with high incomes

12 The opportunity cost of leisure can be defined as the quantity of goods and services which individuals forgo by not working. This being so, the opportunity cost of leisure would fall as a consequence of:

    A   An increase in (wealth) tax on capital transfers
    B   A reduction in the rate of income tax
    C   An increase in the rate of indirect taxes
    D   Introducing a flat-rate poll tax on all individuals

13   Which *one* of the following is an aspect of fiscal policy measures by the government?

A   To raise short-term interest rates in the money markets
B   To support the exchange rate for the country's currency
C   To control growth in the money supply
D   To alter rates of taxation

14   'Supply side' economics concerns:

A   The behaviour of the microeconomic supply curve

B   The supply of factors of production in response to changing levels of factor rewards

C   The behaviour of the aggregate supply curve in connection with the levels of prices, incomes and employment

D   The effect that an increase in the supply of money has on inflation

15   If a government wishes to increase consumer spending, it could increase the rate of:

A   Income tax
B   Corporation tax
C   Import duties
D   Social security payments

16   The concept of liquidity preference refers to

A   People's preference for equity rather than debt
B   People's preference to hold their savings as cash rather than investing them
C   Banks' preference for short-term lending rather than long-term lending
D   Banks' preference for equity rather than debt

17   Which of the following are true:

(i)   If interest rates are low but expected to rise, liquidity preference will be high
(ii)   If interest rates are high but expected to fall, liquidity preference will be high
(iii)   The demand for money is high when interest rates are low
(iv)   The demand for money is high when interest rates are high

A   (i) only
B   (ii) only
C   (i) and (iii)
D   (ii) and (iv)

18   If a country has 10 million spending transactions per year, at an average price of $50, and the annual velocity of circulation is 4, what is its money supply?

A $100 million
B $125 million
C $150 million
D $200 million

19   Which one of the following would monetarist economists not agree with?

    A   An increase in the money supply will lead to an increase in the level of inflation

    B   Fiscal policies are the most effective at reducing unemployment in the long run

    C   The level of government borrowing should be reduced or controlled because a budget deficit will lead to an increase in the money supply

    D   The level of the public sector net cash requirement (PSNCR) should be controlled because a large PSNCR will lead to the crowding out of private sector investment.

20   Which one of the following would be likely to occur if there was an increase in the money supply in an economy?

    A   A rise in the rate of inflation
    B   A rise in interest rates
    C   A rise in exchange rates
    D   A fall in the levels of investment

21   What is the public sector net cash requirement (PSNCR)?

22   If a government wants to exercise an expansionary fiscal policy it should

    A   Reduce taxes; increase government expenditure
    B   Increase taxes; reduce government expenditure
    C   Increase money supply; reduce government expenditure
    D   Reduce money supply; increase government expenditure

Chapter 13(a)

International trade – the foreign exchange market

This set of questions covers Chapter 13(a) of the BPP Study Text for Paper C4, looking at how foreign exchange rates are determined and their impact on business.

1   A spot rate is the rate set for the delivery of currency

    A   At some future date
    B   Now
    C   Tomorrow
    D   In three months

2   A forward rate is

    A   The future spot rate of the currency
    B   The rate for delivery of the currency at some future date
    C   The rate set for immediate delivery of the currency
    D   The rate set by the central bank

3   The Purchasing Power Parity Theory predicts that the exchange value of a currency depends on

    A   The relative level of interest rates
    B   Relative prices
    C   The relative size of trade deficits
    D   The relative size of budget deficits

4   Le Bleu, a company based in France, has just received \$500,000 on a contract it undertook in the US. The current €/\$ exchange rate is 0.8000 – 0.8100.

    Le Bleu's receipts in Euros will be ☐

5   The current inflation rate in the US is running at 6% and 5% in the UK. The exchange rate between the two countries is 1.7800 \$/£. If exchange rates adjust to keep purchasing power unchanged in each country, the exchange rate in one year's time will be

    A   1.6952
    B   1.7632
    C   1.7970
    D   1.8690

6   The interest rate parity condition relates differences between spot and forward exchange rates to:

   A   The relative inflation rates in the two countries
   B   The relative interest rates in the two countries
   C   The relative trade deficits in the two countries
   D   The relative budget deficits in the two countries

7   The current exchange rate between the US and the UK is 1.7500 $/£. The current central bank lending rates are 4% in the US and 6% in the UK. What will the predicted forward exchange rate be for a year's time ?

   A   Above the spot rate
   B   Below the spot rate
   C   Same as the spot rate
   D   Cannot tell

8   Which of the following is a disadvantage of floating exchange rates?

   A   Balance of payments deficits or surpluses are automatically corrected
   B   Currency risk is maximised
   C   Governments do not have to hold foreign currency reserves
   D   There is no conflict with other economic policies

9   Which of the following is not an advantage of a single currency?

   A   Elimination of currency risk
   B   Price transparency
   C   Free movement of capital
   D   Same interest rate

10   Transaction risk arises when the prices of imports or exports are fixed in foreign currency terms and there is a change in......................................between the date the price is agreed and the date when the transaction takes place.

   A   Exchange rates
   B   Inflation rates
   C   Interest rates
   D   The trade deficit

11   Which of the following would be expected to lead to a fall in the value of £ sterling against the US dollar?

   (i)   A rise in US Interest rates
   (ii)   A rise in UK interest rates
   (iii) Intervention by the Bank of England to buy sterling

   A   (i) only
   B   (ii) only
   C   (i) and (iii)
   D   (ii) and (iii)

12   If a country's central bank increases the supply of its currency on to the market, what is likely to happen to the country's foreign exchange rate (*ceteribus peribus*) ?

13   A fixed exchange rate is not normally compatible in the long term with different inflation rates in the countries concerned.

☐   True

☐   False

14   Fill in the gaps.

A marked deterioration in the UK's balance of trade is likely to lead to..
.... in the value of sterling. There will be .... need to buy foreign currency to pay for imports.

A   A decrease; decreased

B   A decrease; increased

C   An increase; decreased

D   An increase; increased

15   The main advantage of a system of flexible (floating) exchange rates is that it:

A   Provides certainty for international traders

B   Provides automatic correction of balance of payments deficits

C   Reduces international transactions costs

D   Provides policy discipline for governments

16   A fixed exchange rate is unlikely to be put under pressure by:

A   Capital movements

B   Trade in goods and services

C   Falling unemployment

D   Speculation

17   Which one of the following is not a benefit from countries forming a monetary union and adopting a single currency?

A   International transaction costs are reduced

B   Exchange rate uncertainly is removed

C   It reduces the need for foreign exchange reserves

D   It allows each country to adopt an independent monetary policy

18   Which *one* of the following is a characteristic of floating (flexible) exchange rates?

A   They provide automatic correction for balance of payments deficits and surpluses

B   They reduce uncertainty for businesses

C   Transactions costs involved in exchanging currencies are eliminated

D   They limit the ability of governments to adopt expansionary policies

19 On the currency markets, a spot rate is valid for immediate delivery only.

☐ True
☐ False

20 Insert the missing word in the sentence below.

The major disadvantage of a single currency system like the Eurozone is that member countries lose all

control over .... policy.

A   Fiscal
B   Monetary

21 Which one of the following must always balance?

A   Balance of trade
B   Balance of payments current account
C   Balance of payments
D   Balance of payments financial account

22 Devaluation of the currency will:

A   Improve the terms of trade and *not* increase the cost of living.
B   Improve the terms of trade but increase the cost of living.
C   Worsen the terms of trade but *not* increase the cost of living.
D   Worsen the terms of trade and increase the cost of living.

23 If there were an excessive outflow of sterling from the UK, which of the following would you expect to happen?

A   The UK's terms of trade would improve.
B   There would be a revaluation of sterling.
C   Interest rates would fall.
D   There would be a fall in the exchange value of sterling.

24 Suppose that demand for imports in the UK is inelastic. If sterling were to depreciate in value against other countries, which of the following would happen?

	Imports would become	*Total spending by the UK on imports*
A	Cheaper in £ sterling	Would rise
B	Cheaper in £ sterling	Would fall
C	More expensive in £ sterling	Would rise
D	More expensive in £ sterling	Would fall

✓

25 Gerdaland is a country for which the demand for imports is price inelastic, and the demand for its exports is price elastic. If Gerdaland's domestic currency appreciates in value, which of the following will happen?

A   Exports will increase in value and imports will fall in value.
B   Exports will increase in value and imports will increase in value.
C   Exports will fall in value and imports will fall in value.
D   Exports will fall in value and imports will increase in value.

26 Demand for imports in a country is inelastic and demand for the country's exports is also inelastic in response to price changes. The country's government raises interest rates substantially, and interest rates in other countries remain unchanged. The consequences of the higher interest rates should be:

A   Higher total imports; higher total exports
B   Lower total imports; higher total exports
C   Higher total imports; lower total exports
D   Lower total imports; lower total exports

Chapter 13(b)

International trade – the international economy

This set of questions covers Chapter 13(b) of the BPP Study Text for Paper C4, looking at the rationale for international trade and how it affects the national economies of countries participating in it.

1   A country has a comparative advantage over another country when it can produce more of a good from a given amount of resources.

☐ True
☐ False

2   Country X and Country Y each produce both guns and butter. Using the same total amount of resources to produce either guns or butter, the two countries can achieve the output shown below.

	Guns	Butter (tons)
Country X	20	200
Country Y	10	150

According to the law of comparative advantage (comparative costs), should Country Y import guns or butter from Country X?

☐ Guns
☐ Butter

3   Dumping is a form of trade protection in which onerous administrative requirements are imposed in order to hamper importers.

☐ True
☐ False

4   A regional trading bloc must use a single currency for its transactions.

☐ True
☐ False

5   Which of the following is not a characteristic of a common market?

A   Harmonisation of levels of direct taxation
B   Common external tariffs
C   Free trade among members
D   Free movement of factors of production between member countries

6   Complete the sentences below.

A rise in interest rates will enlarge a .... on the balance of trade. The rise in interest rates will lead to a .... in the exchange rate, which will make exports .... and imports..

A   Surplus; rise; cheaper; more expensive
B   Deficits; fall; more expensive; cheaper
C   Surplus; fall; cheaper; more expensive
D   Deficit; rise; more expensive; cheaper

7   Name the axes of the J curve shown below.

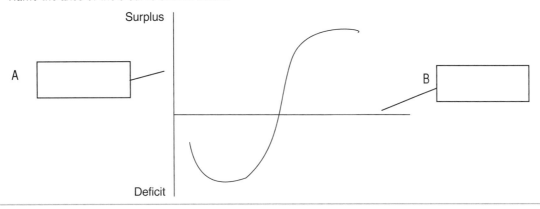

8   The comparative cost model of international trade shows that trade arises because of differences between countries in:

A   The absolute costs of production
B   Patterns of consumer demand
C   The opportunity costs of production
D   The structure of production

9   A tariff restriction imposed on the flow of imports into a country would be expected to lead to all of the following *except* which one?

A   An improvement in the trade balance
B   A reduction in unemployment
C   Reduced competition for domestic producers
D   A fall in the rate of inflation

10   The theory of comparative advantage suggests that countries should:

A   Diversify their production as much as possible
B   Engage in trade if the opportunity costs of production differ between countries
C   Engage in trade only if each country has an absolute advantage in at least one good or service
D   Aim to make their economies self-sufficient

11   Which *one* of the following is *not* an economic advantage of international trade?

A   It encourages international specialisation.
B   Consumer choice is widened.
C   It enables industries to secure economies of large-scale production.
D   Trade surpluses can be used to finance the budget deficit.

12   Which of the following policies for correcting a balance of payments deficit is an expenditure-reducing policy?

A   Cutting the level of public expenditure
B   Devaluation of the currency
C   The imposition of an import tax
D   The use of import quotas

13   A multi-national company is best described as one which:

A   Engages extensively in international trade
B   Sells its output in more than one country
C   Produces goods or services in more than one country
D   Is owned by shareholders in more than one country

14   Which of the following is most likely to cause a country's balance of payments to move towards a deficit?

A   A devaluation of that country's currency
B   An expansionary fiscal policy
C   A contractionary fiscal policy
D   A rise in the rate of domestic saving

15   Which of the following are benefits accruing to countries which adopt a single currency, such as the Euro?

(i)   Reduced exchange rates uncertainty
(ii)   Reduction in balance of payments deficit
(iii)   Increased price transparency
(iv)   Lower interest rates

A   (i), (ii) and (iii)
B   (i), (iii) and (iv)
C   (i) and (iii)
D   (ii) and (iv)

16   A favourable movement in the terms of trade for a country means that:

A   The balance of trade has improved
B   The volume of exports has risen relative to the volume of imports
C   The prices of exports have risen relative to the prices of imports
D   The revenue from exports has risen relative to the revenue from imports

17 Which one of the following *cannot* be used to finance a deficit on the current account of a country's balance of payments?

A Running down foreign exchange reserves
B Increased taxation
C Borrowing from foreign central banks
D Attracting inflows of short-term capital

18 The imposition of which *one* of the following would *not* act as a barrier to international trade?

A A value added tax
B Tariffs
C Import quotas
D Exchange controls

19 Globalisation of capital markets is due to:

A International trade in commodities
B International trade in microchips
C Increasing numbers of expatriate managers
D Increasing financial deregulation

20 All of the following are problems of managing international businesses *except* which *one*?

A The J-curve effect
B Management style
C Measuring performance
D Staffing

21 A currency devaluation is likely to produce a J-curve effect if:

A The terms of trade worsen
B Supply and demand are elastic
C The terms of trade improve
D Supply and demand are inelastic

22 Which of the following is likely to be associated with an improvement in a country's terms of trade?

A Increasing levels of imports
B Investment producing more sophisticated products
C Increasing levels of exports
D Investment in cheaper overseas production facilities

23 Assume that two small countries, X and Y, produce two commodities P and Q, and that there are no transport costs. One unit of resource in Country X produces 4 units of P or 8 units of Q. One unit of resource in Country Y produces 1 unit of P or 3 units of Q.

Which *one* of the following statements is *true*?

A Country X has an absolute advantage over Country Y in producing P and Q, and so will not trade.
B Country X does not have an absolute advantage over Country Y in producing P and Q.
C Country Y has a comparative advantage over Country X in producing Q.
D Country X has a comparative advantage over Country Y in producing both P and Q.

24 The J curve effect prevents devaluation from having a long term effect on a country's balance of trade.

☐ True
☐ False

25 Which of the following would *not* be a feature of globalisation?

A Increased international capital flows
B Transnational mergers
C Increased number of multi-national firms
D Increased independence of national economies

26 A country's balance of trade is determined by the prices of its imports and exports.

☐ True
☐ False

27 Complete the sentence.

The .... condition states that in order for a reduction in the exchange rate to reduce a country's balance of payments deficit, the sum of the price elasticities of demand and supply must be .... than 1.

A Phillips; greater
B Phillips; less
C Marshall-Lerner; greater
D Marshall-Lerner; less

28 Bonjovia's terms of trade have declined in 20X6 to 80% of their 20X5 value.

Index numbers for import and export prices for the two years are given below.

What is the missing index number?

	Exports	Imports
20X5	150	☐
20X6	144	216

29 The effect of a change in a country's terms of trade on its balance of payments will depend on the price elasticity of demand of both its imports and its exports.

☐ True
☐ False

30 The table below shows the production capability on one unit of resource in each of two countries, in terms of producing cars and rice.

	Cars		Rice
Bandia	3	or	45 tonnes
Sparta	10	or	60 tonnes

Assume that there are no transport costs, and that opportunity costs are constant for all levels of output. The law of comparative advantage would predict that:

A Bandia will export rice and Sparta will export cars
B Sparta will export rice and Bandia will export cars
C Sparta will export both rice and cars
D Sparta will export cars and there will be no trade in rice between the countries

31 From a given base year, a country's export prices rise by 8% and import prices rise by 20%. During this period, the terms of trade will have:

A Risen from 100 to 111.1
B Risen from 100 to 112
C Fallen from 100 to 90
D Fallen from 100 to 88

32 Which of the following items would *not* be included in the UK Balance of Payments statistics?

A The terms of trade
B The takeover of a UK company by a Swiss company
C Investments overseas by UK individuals
D UK government borrowing from International Monetary Fund

33 Which of the following financial transactions will have an adverse effect on the UK's balance of payments current account, at least in the short run?

1 Increased tourism abroad by UK residents
2 Increased private export of investment capital abroad
3 The payment of cash grant to a developing country by the UK government

A Item 1 only
B Items 1 and 2 only
C Items 1 and 3 only
D Items 2 and 3 only

34   If the level of real incomes of the population in the UK were to rise, the UK's balance of payments position would worsen because:

A   The UK's terms of trade would worsen
B   Export prices would rise
C   Import volumes would rise
D   Sterling would appreciate in value

35   The government of a certain country embarks on a policy of reflating the economy. At the same time, it uses its control over interest rates to maintain the stability of the exchange rate for the country's currency. For which of the following reasons might the country's balance of payments go into deficit in the short term?

1   Manufacturers divert goods that would otherwise be exported into domestic markets
2   Foreign investors, attracted by the economic reflation, invest money in the country
3   Economic expansion raises aggregate demand in the economy, so that demand for imports rises

A   Reasons 1 and 2 only
B   Reasons 1 and 3 only
C   Reasons 2 and 3 only
D   Reasons 3 only

36   According to the law of comparative advantage, the consequences of protectionism in international trade are that protectionist measures will prevent:

A   Each country of the world from maximising its economic wealth
B   Each country of the world from maximising the value of its exports
C   The countries of the world from maximising their total output with their economic resources
D   Each country of the world from achieving equilibrium in its balance of payments

37   In two countries, Lornga and Ziortia, the production of wheat and beef from a given input of factors is as follows.

Lornga: 18 units of wheat or 6 units of beef
Ziortia: 9 units of wheat or 3 units of beef

From this data, it can be deduced that:

A   Both countries can benefit from international trade in wheat and beef, because of comparative advantage

B   Ziortia cannot benefit from trade in wheat or beef with Lornga, because Ziortia is less efficient in producing both

C   Lornga cannot benefit from trade in wheat with Ziortia, because Ziortia's unit costs for wheat will be higher

D   Neither country can benefit from trade because their opportunity cost are the same

38   Which of the following items would be in the UK balance of trade statistics?

1   Tourist spending in the UK
2   Accountancy services performed by firms of UK auditors in Germany
3   Timber imported from Scandinavia and re-exported to Spain

A   Items 1 and 2 only
B   Items 1 and 3 only
C   Items 2 and 3 only
D   Item 3 only

39   A country's electronics industry, which is its major export industry, switches from the production of mass low-cost, low-profit margin microchips to the production of more high-powered, high-cost, high-profit margin custom-built microchips. The consequence of this switch in production for the country will be:

A   An improvement in the balance of trade
B   A deterioration in the balance of trade
C   An improvement in the terms of trade
D   A deterioration the terms of trade

40   The UK balance of payments (on current account) will be worsened by all of the following *except* which *one*?

A   A reduction in spending by overseas tourists in the UK
B   A reduction in the overseas earnings of UK banks
C   A reduction in investment in the UK by foreign firms
D   An increase in the amount of dividends paid by UK subsidiaries of foreign multinational companies

41   Inflation in a country's economy has led to a deterioration in the balance of payments current account. Which of the following reasons might explain this?

1   The terms of trade have worsened due to the higher export prices.
2   Higher domestic prices have made imported goods more attractive.
3   Excess demand in domestic markets has reduced the volume of goods available for export.

A   Reasons 1 and 2 only
B   Reasons 1 and 3 only
C   Reason 2 only
D   Reasons 2 and 3 only

42   Which of the following is a feature of an economic and monetary union, but not a common market?

A   Free movement of goods and services between countries
B   Free markets in each of the factors of production
C   A common external tariff
D   A single currency

43   A country's terms of trade improve. Which of the following implications will *necessarily* apply?

     1   The balance of payments on current account will now improve.
     2   The exchange rate will now appreciate in value.
     3   Export prices will already have risen.

     A   Implications 1 and 2 only
     B   Implications 1 and 3 only
     C   Implications 2 and 3 only
     D   None of them necessarily applies

44   A country has a balance of trade equal to zero and high imports and exports relative to the size of its National Income. There is then a depreciation of its currency. What will be the consequence or consequences of this depreciation of the currency?

     1   It will improve the terms of trade.
     2   It will improve the balance of trade if the demand for both exports and imports is inelastic.
     3   It might lead to cost-push inflation.

     A   Consequences 1 and 2 only
     B   Consequences 1 and 3 only
     C   Consequences 2 and 3 only
     D   Consequence 3 only

45   Denland has the following trade account figures for 20X6:

	$m
Trade in goods (net position of exports minus imports)	−400
Trade in services (net position of exports minus imports)	250
Income *from* capital investment overseas	150
Transfers *to* overseas bodies	−125
Balance of capital flows in the capital account	50
Balance of investment flows on the financial account	70
Net errors and omissions	5

     The balance on Denland's balance of payments current account for 20X6 was:

     A   −$150m
     B   −$125m
     C   Zero
     D $125m

Answers

Chapter 1(a)

1 (i)   Land   Rent
   (ii) Labour   Wages
   (iii) Capital   Interest
   (iv) Enterprise Profit

2 In a command economy, decisions about resource allocation are made by the **government**.

3 Economic costs are also referred to as **opportunity costs**, being the costs of losing the opportunity to undertake a different course of action.

4 Normal profit is the opportunity cost of the owner's money and time and the opportunity cost of **capital** which could have been put to alternative use.

5 The cost of an item measured in terms of the alternatives foregone is called its **opportunity cost**.

6 True Economic profit takes into account the normal rate of return for the equity capital that is required or that could be earned by alternative use for the same level of risk undertaken (the opportunity cost of capital).

7 In a **mixed economy**, economic decisions are made partly by free market forces of supply and demand, and partly by government decisions.

8 D The basic economic problem is one of allocating scarce resources and economics is the study of how those scarce resources are or should be used.

9 D This is a definition of opportunity cost.

10 D The opportunity costs represent the alternative work which is foregone to provide the vaccination programme.

11 C Point C is outside the production possibility frontier and so is not attainable with the current level of resources available.

12 A This is merely a use of production; the other three options will increase the production capacity in the country.

13 C Management is a specialised type of labour. A, B and D are factors of production; the missing factor is **land**.

14 A Fantasia currently produces 13,000 guns and 4,000 tons of butter. If production of guns were reduced to 9,000 and all resources were used effectively, production of butter would rise to about 6,700 tons, an increase of 2,700 tons.

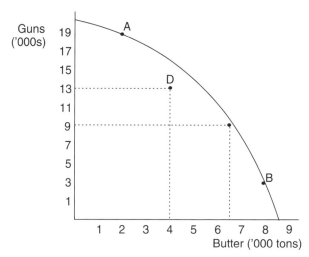

15   D   The production possibility curve is a theoretical maximum: many factors may prevent an economy from achieving its theoretical maximum output. One of these is unemployment, which is, effectively, a failure to use all the available labour resources. A fall in unemployment will thus push output closer to its potential but will not increase that potential. Changes in prices may take effect through the macroeconomy to affect the level of actual output via complex mechanisms, but they cannot in themselves change the potential level of output.

16   D   All of the changes should shift the frontier outwards.

17   C   'Normal profit' is earned by companies in conditions of perfect competition and represents compensation for the risks borne by the entrepreneur or provider of capital.

18   C   In a market economy, decision and choices about resource allocation are determined by the market forces of supply and demand, and the workings of the price mechanism. Option A is describes a command economy; option D describes a mixed economy.

19   B   Secondary sector industries manufacture goods. Service industries form the tertiary sector.

20   D   The correct answer should be: Land is rewarded with rent.

Chapter 1(b)

1   B   The Board of Directors. The principal-agent problem underlines the need for corporate governance in an organisation.

2   The three types of stakeholder in an organisation are **internal**, **external** and **connected**.

3   D   A company's directors are appointed by shareholders.

4   A   The agency or principal-agent problem

5   A   A planned economy or command economy is one in which economic decisions about resource application are taken by a central body, the 'state'. It is in free market economies and mixed economies that factors B, C and D influence resource allocation.

6   B   Much production is likely to be in private ownership.

7   B   It is probably impossible to have a mixed economy without a democracy and *vice versa*, but democracy is a political term while mixed economy is an economic one. A market economy (option C), strictly speaking, has no place for government intervention, as for instance in the provision of welfare. A common market (option D) is an international free trade area with a common external tariff and free movement within it of the factors of production.

8   The sum of the cash flows to contributors of capital to the firm including shareholders and bond holders is the free cash flow to the *firm*. Bond holders are holders of debt, not equity.

9   Free cash flows to equity is a measure of what a firm can afford to pay out as **dividends**.

10   B   A negative NPV indicates future cash flows do not cover the cost of the investment so it should not be undertaken.

11   When using a valuation model to value shares, any increase in the required rate of return will cause the share valuation to **decrease**.

This is because the denominator in the formula has increased.

12   A share valuation will fall as the risk of cash flows **increases**.

Increased risk will require an increased return on capital, therefore reducing the share valuation for the same reason in the previous question.

13

	$
PBIT	4,000,000
– Interest expenses	(400,000)
PBT	3,600,000
– Taxes	(170,000)
Net Income	3,430,000
– Preferred Dividends	(500,000)
Earnings	2,930,000
No of shares	10,000,000
EPS	0.293

14

	$
PBIT	4,000,000
Taxes	(170,000)
Capital Expenditure	(600,000)
Free cash flow to firm	3,230,000

15

	$
PBIT	4,000,000
Taxes	(170,000)
Capital expenditure	(600,000)
Interest expenses	(400,000)
Free cash flow to equity	2,830,000

16 Capital Employed = Assets − Current liabilities = 50,000,000 − 10,000,000 = 40,000,000

ROCE = PBIT/Capital employed = 4,000,000/40,000,000 = 10%

17 ROCE $= \dfrac{\text{Profit before interest and tax}}{\text{Capital employed}}$

$= \dfrac{\$29m}{\$87m} = 0.33$

18 Earnings per share $= \dfrac{\text{Profit after tax and preference dividends}}{\text{Number of equity shares in issue}}$

$= \dfrac{\$18m}{15m}$ (being $29m − $3m − $8m)

$= \$1.20$

19 P/E ratio $= \dfrac{\text{Market price per share}}{\text{Earnings per share}}$

$= \dfrac{\$6.00}{\$1.20} = 5$

20 D Managers have a fiduciary responsibility (or duty of faithful service) to run their business in the way that best serves the business' purpose.

Chapter 2

1 **Fixed costs** remain constant regardless of the level of production while **variable costs** increase in direct proportion to an increase in output.

2 1 D $\dfrac{\text{Total Cost}}{\text{Total Output}}$ = Average Total Costs

2 C $\dfrac{\text{Total Fixed Cost}}{\text{Total Output}}$ = Average Fixed Costs

3 A $\dfrac{\text{Total Cost − Fixed Cost}}{\text{Total Output}}$ = Average Variable cost

4 B $\dfrac{\text{Change in Total Cost}}{\text{Change in Output}}$ = Marginal cost

3   A   II   Marginal cost
     B   I   Average total cost
     C   IV   Average variable cost
     D   III   .Average fixed cost

4   D   Economic profit. Accounting profit only includes explicit costs. Economic profit also includes implicit costs (opportunity costs).

5   B   Economic costs are the opportunity costs of the factors of production employed by the firm.

6   D   Accounting profit does not take into account the opportunity cost of equity capital.

7

	Accounting profit $	Economic profit $
Revenue	2,000,000	2,000,000
Less: Explicit costs	(1,200,000)	(1,200,00)
Implicit costs ($120,000 + $60,000)	–	(180,000)
	800,000	620,000

8   A   Marginal cost is the addition to total cost of producing one more unit of output.

9   C   The total of the average fixed cost per unit plus the average variable cost per unit.

10   C   II and IV. Accounting profit only considers costs and so it generally greater than economy profit which considers both implicit and explicit costs.

11   (a)   Lower
     (b)   Higher

12   D   III and IV. Fixed costs are, by definition, fixed. Whether marginal costs rise or fall depends on the level of output.

13   A   There are economies of scale in production.

14   A   1   Economies of scale
     D   3   Optimal output
     C   2   Diseconomies of scale
     B   4   Constant returns to scale

15   C   Cost curve shifts are caused by changes to the cost of factors of production not changes in demand.

16   True   The fall in average fixed cost as output rises may be sufficient to outweigh a possible increase in average variable cost.

17   External. An example is the existence of a trained and experienced workforce.

18   B   This is a classic example of the operation of diminishing returns.

19   D   Do not confuse the long and short run effects. The long run suffers diseconomies of scale, but diminishing returns are a short run phenomenon.

ANSWERS

20 B Diminishing returns face **all** firms, small and large, in the short run. Large firms should not expand output in the **short run** to a level where diminishing returns are obtained, if they wish to maximise profits. However, in the **longer run**, they can expand without facing diminishing returns at higher output volumes. Do not confuse diminishing returns with diseconomies of scale, which large firms **might** eventually suffer from if they get bigger.

21 B The law of diminishing returns refers to the short run when at least one factor of production is fixed. Since **all** inputs are increased by 50% we must be looking at the long run average cost curve, and in this example, at decreasing returns to scale, since the percentage increase in inputs exceeds the percentage increase in outputs. Decreasing returns to scale will cause the average cost curve to rise.

22 B The others are fixed costs.

23 C Since the MC per unit varies with output (according to the law of diminishing returns) the **average** variable cost for all units produced will not be the same as the marginal cost of the next unit. The other statements are correct: Statement A is true because average fixed costs per unit decline continuously as output increases. Statement D is correct because MC includes normal profit as a cost.

24 D

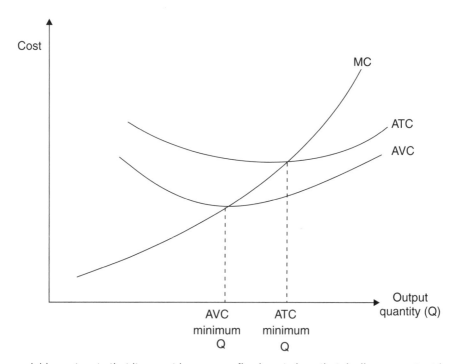

25 Average variable cost: note that it cannot be average fixed cost since that declines as output increases.

26 When the average cost curve is falling, the marginal cost curve will be **below** it. Because the cost of producing one addition is less than the average cost of production this will bring the average down.

27 The law of diminishing returns to scale.

28 False. Economies of scale are a long-run phenomenon. They cause average costs to decline in the long run.

29   D   Technical improvements could apply at any scale of operations.

30   D   Fixed costs are fixed, and both marginal and average variable cost may fall before diminishing returns occur.

31   D

	Cost of 100 units	Cost of 101 units
	$	$
Total variable cost	200	202
Total fixed cost	100	100
Total cost	300	302
Average cost	$3.00	$2.99

The marginal cost is $2, which is the increase in the total variable cost and also the increase in the total cost, since fixed costs are the same at both volumes of output.

32   B   This defines the short run, and the law of diminishing returns is a short run phenomenon.

33   A

	$
Cost of 31 men per hour (× $5.50)	170.50
Cost of 30 men per hour (× $5)	150.00
Marginal cost	20.50

34   C   If the price is less than AVC at the point where MR = MC, the firm would shut down (but not go out of business) if prices are expected to recover in the future. The firm will stop producing in the short run, but will start production once prices have risen. So IV is incorrect.

35   D   Diseconomies of scale are a long run effect. The long run cost curve does not necessarily rise once MES has been reached. Diminishing returns are a short run phenomenon.

36   C   Proposition 3 is false: it is **average** fixed costs per unit (AFC) that fall as output increases. Marginal fixed costs = 0. Since AFC falls, any fall in average variable cost (AVC) must mean a falling average total cost (ATC) since AVC + AFC = ATC. Proposition 2 must therefore also be false.

37   B   Item 2 is an example of an external diseconomy of scale. If an industry grows in size, the competition for resources can push up their cost. For example, skilled labour shortages might occur and push up wage rates. Item 3 is an example of an internal diseconomy of scale. Employees who enjoy working for a smaller firm might become demotivated and less productive as the firm grows into something more bureaucratic and less friendly.

38   B   Marginal cost only considers the variable element of cost, because fixed cost does not change as output increases.

39   D   Minimum efficient scale is the point where long run average costs are at a minimum.

40   A   To the extent that the guard protects society against crime, his costs are a social *benefit* rather than a social *cost*. Statements 1 and 2 are correct, however, for the reasons explained in each statement.

41   C   This question presumes that you know that a perfectly competitive firm can sell all its extra output at the same price as previous output. This means that the extra output will have a higher MRP in a perfectly competitive environment than in the case of Muscles Co, which must reduce its prices, and earn progressively less marginal revenue, to sell more.

42	B	They apply over the long run, when all factors are subject to change.

43 C The company is running the same services as before, and so is not expanding its output and economies of scale are not achieved here. The lower costs per passenger mile will be the result of a reduction in the work force from 8 to just 4.

44 A Market participants can only adapt fully to a change in market conditions in the long run, eg expanding the size of their production facilities. In the short run, supply is relatively inelastic.

45 D When a firm is producing at the lowest point on its average cost curve it is achieving technical efficiency. Allocative efficiency is achieved where price equals marginal cost.

46 B A merger between two firms at different stages in the same production process is an example of vertical integration.

47 B Horizontal integration occurs when two firms in the same business merge.

Chapter 3

1 B In a free market economy, it is the interaction of supply and demand through the price mechanism that determines what should be produced and who should get it.

2 A The supply curve for a perfectly competitive firm is its marginal cost curve above the average variable cost curve. The firm will not continue to produce if price is less than average variable cost.

3 True. In contrast to normal goods which have a downward sloping demand curve, Giffen goods have an upward sloping demand curve.

4 If an increase in the price of a good causes a increase in demand for another good, that good is a **substitute**.

5 If an increase in demand for a good causes an increase in demand for another good, that good is a **complement**.

6 True. Demand for inferior goods falls (and demand for normal goods rises) when household income rises.

7 **Producer surplus** is the difference between the price at which a producer would be prepared to sell a good and the prevailing market price.

8 False. Such goods are **substitutes**; complements are bought and used together.

9 A = 3

B = 1, 2 and 4

10 False. This may affect *demand* if the other goods are complements or substitutes, but not supply.

11 Consumer surplus.

12 D Nothing. A minimum price (floor price) only leads to excess supply if it is set *higher* than the equilibrium price.

13 C The other options relate to movements *along* the supply curve.

14	C	The effect of price being above the equilibrium (market clearing) price is that supply will extend and demand will contract.
15	D	A rise in the price of overseas holidays will lead to a movement along the demand curve rather than a shift in the demand curve.
16	B	Generally, if incomes fall, demand will fall.
17	C	Demand will transfer to the substitute.
18	D	Carpet underlay is a complement to carpet.
19	C	An increase in demand for cars will lead to an increase in demand for petrol, tyres and navigation systems. It will not increase the demand for holidays although people may use their cars to go on holiday.
20	B	This is a supply-side factor.
21	B	A reduction in income tax will increase real household income, and so demand for normal products will shift to the right – quantity demanded will be greater at any given price. Items A and D will cause a leftward shift in the demand curve. Item C would cause a movement to the right along the demand curve.
22	D	Coffee and tea are substitute products. Thus, a fall in the price of coffee will result in higher demand for coffee and lower demand for its substitute product, tea. The price of tea might therefore fall. Demand for drinking cups is probably insufficiently related to the consumption of coffee to make them a complementary product to coffee. Even so, lower coffee prices would be likely to raise the demand for drinking cups rather than reduce it.
23	D	The term 'inferior good' is a technical term in economics. An example of such a good might be small 'starter' homes.
24	D	It is assumed that cut flowers and flower vases are complementary goods. The rise in price of cut flowers will have an adverse effect on demand for flower vases, and the demand curve for flower vases will shift to the left. Given no change in supply conditions for vases, the new equilibrium price for vases will be lower.
25	B	As sea ferry tickets and hovercraft tickets are substitute goods, an increase in the price of hovercraft tickets will cause a shift to the right (increase in demand) for sea ferry tickets. Given no change in supply conditions, the consequence will be an increase in the number of sea ferry tickets sold, at a higher price than before.
26	A	A fall in the price of **sterling** would make London hotels cheaper for foreign tourists. A fall in the price of aeroplane tickets would make London cheaper to visit for foreign tourists. Events 2 and 3 would lead to a **rise** in demand for hotel rooms. In contrast, a fall in the value of the US dollar would make the UK more expensive to visit for US tourists and tourists from other countries where the US dollar is widely used, and demand for hotel rooms in London would fall.
27	C	A demand curve shifts to the left when demand for the good at any given price level is less than before. Changes 2 and 4 both have this effect, although Change 4 applies to normal goods, **not** to inferior goods. Change 1 causes a movement along the existing demand curve. Change 3 causes a shift to the **right** of the demand curve.

28   B   When rent controls are eased, the effect is similar to raising or removing minimum prices in the rented housing market. We should expect higher rents, more supply of housing, and a closing of the gap between demand for rented housing and supply of rented accommodation. Changes 2 and 3 should therefore occur. The reverse of Change 1 should happen, and homelessness should decrease. Given widespread homelessness, it is unlikely that the easing of rent controls will have any effect on demand for owner-occupied dwellings.

29   D   All of the above.

30   B   The demand curve here indicates the marginal benefit that consumers receive from purchasing an additional unit. Assuming consumers are rational, the level of marginal benefit they receive will determine the maximum price they are prepared to pay for an additional unit.

31   B   A change in the price of a good will lead to a movement along the supply curve, not a shift in the curve itself.

32   C   As costs incurred in a producing sofas have fallen, producers will be prepared to produce more at any given price. A change in the price of sofas will lead to a movement along the supply curve. A decrease in the price of a substitute will lead to a decrease in the demand for sofas.

33   B   Although there is a surplus, this does not mean that the good is no longer scarce. At the current price, however, buyers desire less of a good than sellers want to bring to the market so there is a surplus. Scarcity indicates that a good is less freely available than consumers would like.

34   A   Consumer surplus is the excess between what consumers are prepared to pay for a good or service and the prevailing market price they have to pay to purchase it.

35   C   In the short run, firms will continue to supply provided that they cover variable costs. They will incur fixed costs whether they produce any output or not. Therefore provided revenues cover variable costs and therefore make a contribution towards fixed costs, it is beneficial for the firm to continue producing.

36   B   A rise in household incomes will lead to a shift in the demand curve, not the supply curve.

37   The introduction of a government subsidy will cause the supply curve to shift to the right (outwards).

38   (i)   A change in household incomes: Shift in demand curve
      (ii)   A change in the price of raw materials: Shift in supply curve
      (iii) A change in consumer tastes: Shift in demand curve
      (iv)   The imposition of a floor price: Neither

      Options (i) & (iii) represent changes in the conditions of demand. Option (ii) is a change in the conditions of supply. Option (iv) will bring about a price change, but does not affect the conditions of supply or demand.

39   Goods A and B are complements.

40   Goods A and B are substitutes.

Chapter 4

1   Demand is inelastic

% change in Q = $\dfrac{2}{10}$ = 20%

% change in P = $\dfrac{1.0}{2.5}$ = 40%

PED = $\dfrac{20\%}{40\%}$ = 0.5

$OR\ \dfrac{\Delta Q}{Q} \times \dfrac{P}{\Delta P} = \dfrac{2}{10} \times \dfrac{2.5}{1} = \dfrac{5}{10}$ = 0.5

2   Fall.

3   False. Demand would rise. A Giffen good has an upward sloping demand curve.

4   (i)   The formula for calculating cross elasticity of demand is: $\dfrac{\%\ \text{change in quantity demanded of good A}}{\%\ \text{change in price of good B}}$

       (ii)   Substitutes.

5   B   The supply curve is a straight line passing through the origin when the supply of goods has unit elasticity.

6   D   Demand is perfectly inelastic if a change in price has no impact on the quality demanded.

7   More. Consumption patterns take time to alter since it takes time for suppliers to provide substitutes and for consumers to become aware of their availability.

8   True   If demand for the end product is inelastic, the cost of wage increase can be passed on to the end consumer but, if demand is elastic, it cannot.

9   A   With unit elasticity of demand, total revenue does not change for different price levels, but the same cannot be said about profit. Elasticity of demand tells us nothing about a firm's cost structure.

10   B   Price elasticity of demand = −2.5

         Price elasticity of demand = $\dfrac{\%\ \text{change in quality demanded}}{\%\ \text{change in price}} = \dfrac{5{,}000/20{,}000}{-2/20} = \dfrac{25\%}{10\%} = -2.5$

11   B   The size of the elasticity is then greater than 1.

12   B   The elasticity of supply of the final product will not be an influencing factor.

13   A   **Statement 1** is incorrect. When demand is price elastic, a fall in price will *increase* total spending on the good. **Statement 2** is incorrect, because when household income rises, demand for an inferior good will fall: income elasticity of demand will be negative, not zero. **Statement 3** is incorrect. If goods A and B are complements, a rise in the price of B will cause a fall in the demand for A, and so cross elasticity of demand is negative.

14   A   Statement A is correct: demand will tend to be elastic when the product has a large number of close substitutes. The rate of consumption (statement B) could be irrelevant to elasticity. However, a high *rate* of demand/consumption might suggest consumer goods, which tend to have elastic demand. Statement C is incorrect. If a product is bought by people on subsistence incomes, a rise in its price is unlikely to result in higher total spending on the product (ie demand will *not* be inelastic) and if demand switches to cheaper substitutes, which is likely, demand for the product will be price elastic. Luxury goods (statement D) tend to be price elastic.

15   A   Widgets and splodgets are complements. When the price of splodgets goes up by 10%, demand for widgets will go **down** by ($\times$ 0.6) 6% at that price. The demand curve for widgets has shifted to the left, and a new equilibrium price and output quantity will be established, at a lower output and price. However, since we do not know what the supply curve for widgets is, we cannot say what the new equilibrium price will be.

16   B   A rise in the price of a good bought by people on subsistence incomes is likely to make them switch their buying to other (substitute) products, and so demand for the good will tend to be elastic. A fall in the price of the product will have a reverse effect, making consumers demand significantly more of the product since it is now relatively cheaper than before, compared to the price of substitutes.

17   B

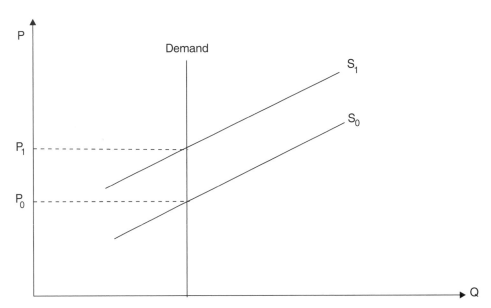

The effect of the increase in tax is to shift the supply curve from S_0 to S_1, the vertical difference between S_0 and S_1 being the amount of the tax. The price change, from P_0 to P_1, is the amount of the tax, which is fully borne by the consumer. Demand volume remains unchanged.

18   B   Oddly enough, advertising (a form of non-price competition) is more likely to be successful for products with a low price elasticity of demand – ie for products whose demand is influenced by factors other than price. **Statements A and D** are incorrect because the supply curves of the product will be unaffected. **Statement C** is not necessarily correct because the higher total profits (and revenue) from their higher price will not necessarily cover the costs of the advertising.

19   D   When price elasticity of demand is 1, total revenue remains unchanged following a change in price. This means that MR must be zero (since any change in output will leave revenue the same), and that total revenue must be at a maximum (since any change in price/output will leave revenue the same). Statement 2 is wrong, since the average revenue (ie price) must change with output for total revenue to remain unchanged.

20   C

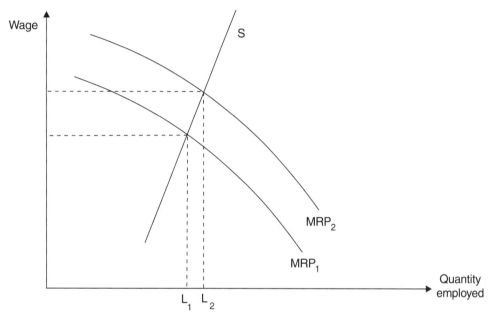

The diagram shows that a shift in the MRP of labour due to productivity improvements, from MRP_1 to MRP_2, will result in a relatively small increase in employment numbers from L_1 to L_2 and a relatively large increase in wages from W_1 to W_2.

21   D   The demand for the good will be highly price inelastic. We would need details about the good to know if it was either 'inferior' or a luxury good.

22   A   If price rises, total revenue rises. This is a defining characteristic of inelastic demand

23   D   Since elasticity of demand = 1, the total revenue from selling an extra unit would remain unchanged (the quantity sold would fall) and MR = 0. Since MC = $25, there would be an incremental loss of $25.

24   C   The supply curve for labour will be more elastic for a single firm than for the industry as a whole.

25   A   This is best illustrated by a diagram.

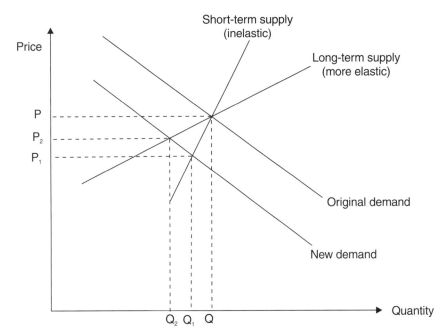

The original equilibrium is price P and output Q. When demand falls, supply will fall in the short run to Q_1 and the price will fall to P_1. In the longer term, supply capacity is reduced, and the supply curve becomes more elastic. The output quantity falls further to Q_2, and price recovers to P_2, which is less than the original equilibrium price P.

26   C   Cross elasticity of demand = $\dfrac{\text{\% change in quantity of good A demanded *}}{\text{\% change in the price of good B}}$

*given no change in the price of A

If Smudge Paints puts its prices up, we should expect customers to switch to buying more from Dogsbrush; hence cross elasticity of demand is positive. Since the products are in direct competition with each other, the cross elasticity of demand should be high.

27   B   A demand curve falling elasticity as you move downwards to the right (ie as quantity increases)

28   C

P1 = $3, Q1 = 20,000

P2 = $2.60, Q2 = 25,000

% change in quantity demanded $= \dfrac{Q_1 - Q_2}{\left(Q_1 + Q_2\right) \div 2} = \dfrac{5,000}{45,000 \div 2} = 0.222$

% change in price $= \dfrac{-0.40}{(5.60 \div 2)} = -0.143$

Price elasticity of demand $= \dfrac{\text{\% change in quantity}}{\text{\% change in price}} = \dfrac{0.222}{-0.143} = -1.55$

29 B Total revenue will increase as the price is dropped on the elastic portion of the demand curve. Marginal revenue is falling across the length of the demand curve.

30 B I, II, III and IV are all correct.

31 A The cobweb effect. This is a definition.

32 A The number of substitutes, and the proportion of income spent on a good are major determinants of its price elasticity of demand. Options 3 & 4 will lead to a shift in the demand curve, but they will not in themselves affect the elasticity of demand.

Chapter 5

1 False. Externalities are one of the *aspects* of market failure, but they are not the cause of it. The term 'market imperfection' in economics describes any market where perfect competition is not present.

2 An externality.

3 B The consumer bears increase AC. The producers incur the cost CB.

4 C This is related to the trade cycle.

5 A Health and education are merit goods. Defence and street lighting are public goods.

6 B Social cost is the sum of the private cost to a firm *plus* the external cost to society as a whole. Here, social cost is the sum of production costs (private costs) plus the cost of pollution (external cost). The firm's private costs might have been increased by the measures to reduce pollution, but the external costs will have fallen, so that total social costs should have fallen too.

7 B The price mechanism has nothing to do with income.

8 C When demand is inelastic, then consumers will not react significantly to a rise in price. Consequently, producers are able to pass much of the price rise on to consumers.

When supply is inelastic, the burden of tax will fall primarily on the producer.

Therefore, when demand is inelastic and supply elastic, the primary burden of a tax will fall most heavily on buyers.

9 D The excess burden of tax or deadweight loss is lower when the imposition of tax does not significantly reduce the number of units traded (ie there is no significant decrease in trade). When demand is inelastic, the deadweight loss is lower as consumers will not react significantly to a rise in prices. When supply is inelastic, the deadweight loss is again lower as producers will not change output levels significantly in response to a price change. As a result, the excess burden of tax is minimized when demand and supply are both inelastic.

10 A By establishing property rights (which may be tradeable), market forces ought to be able to resolve a market failure in the least distortive manner. Floor prices, quotas and subsidies all distort the workings of the price mechanism.

11   A   A public good is one which is indivisible, and so will not be provided by a private company because
         that company would have no way of ensuring that only those people who have paid for the good or
         service benefit from it. Of the four options, this is only true for a national defence system. It would be
         possible to restrict the provision of health, transport and education services to those people who
         have paid for them.

Chapter 6

1   (a)   Increased
    (b)   Higher
    (c)   Equals, profit maximising

2   True   At equilibrium under perfect competition AC = MC = MR = AR = Price, because a firm operating under
           perfect competition has a horizontal demand curve.

3   C   A firm operating under perfect competition is a price taker so faces a horizontal demand curve.
        Therefore price = MR =AR. The equilibrium position (MC = MR) therefore also means that MC = AR.

4   A   In economics, profit maximisation is assumed to be the basic aim for all firms.

5   D   At a profit maximising equilibrium, MR = AR = AC = MC and so MC = MR, AC = AR, MR = AR and MC
        = AR.

6   D   1   Profit is maximised at price P and output Q, because this is where MC = MR.

        2   At this price/output level, average cost equals average revenue. Normal profit is included in
            cost, and so the firm is making normal profits only, but no supernormal profits.

        3   Total revenue is maximised because this is the price/output level where MR = 0.

7   B   *Monopolistic competition: long run equilibrium*

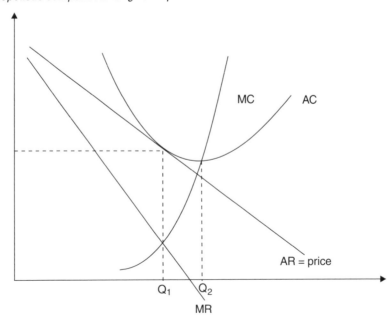

For long run equilibrium in monopolistic competition, MR = MC and AR = AC, but it is **wrong** to say that MR = AC (Statement A) or that AR = MC (Statement D). Since AR = AC, the firm does **not** earn any supernormal profits (Statement C). Statement B is correct because at the profit-maximising output Q_1, average cost is not at a minimum. AC is minimised at output Q_2, which is higher. Since firms could produce more output at a lower AC, we would say that there is excess capacity in the industry.

8   A is marginal revenue, B is average revenue. Remember, marginal revenue can be negative.

9   Maximised.

10   A   The area represents supernormal profit, because average revenue (AR) is greater than average total cost.

11   B   For a firm in a competitive market, average revenue = marginal revenue. The profit maximization rule is marginal revenue = marginal cost

12   B   The firm will produce additional units until it reaches the point where MC = MR. The marginal cost and marginal revenue of each unit is as follows

Unit	Total Variable Cost	Marginal Cost	Total Revenue	Marginal Revenue
1	2.20	2.20	3.00	3.00
2	3.80	1.60	5.00	2.00
3	4.80	1.00	6.30	1.30
4	6.12	1.32	7.20	0.90

Production of the fourth unit would reduce contribution as MC > MR

Alternatively, identify the output level which gives the highest total profit before fixed costs, given by total revenue – total variable costs. This is an output of 3 units, which gives a profit before fixed costs of 1.50 (6.30 – 4.80), whereas 4 units produced gives a profit before fixed costs of 1.08 (7.20 – 6.12)

13   A   In B, C and D, production should be further to the right, where MR exceeds MC.

14   A   In conditions of perfect competition, the firm can sell whatever output it produces at the market price. The demand curve is horizontal, and therefore represents the marginal revenue curve, as well as the average revenue curve (ie price curve).

15   A   Homogeneous. This is one of the defining characteristics of perfect competition.

16   Zero.   The monopolist is a price maker and therefore has downward sloping average and marginal revenue curves. An increase in units sold will increase total revenue for as long as marginal revenue remains positive. MR = 0 is the limit of this process. Once MR become negative selling an extra unit will reduce total revenue.

17   False.   For price discrimination to increase profits, the separate markets must display different elasticities of demand. Otherwise the AR and MR curves are identical and there is, effectively, only one market.

18 False. Such firms are not faced with a prevailing market price because other firms' products are **comparable** rather than **homogeneous**.

19 This is an oligopoly. Non-price competition is one of the characteristics of an oligopoly.

20 The kinked demand curve of oligopoly features a discontinuous **marginal revenue** curve.

21 B Deadweight loss. This is a definition.

22 B Perfect competition requires a homogeneous product. Product differentiation is an important aspect of monopolistic competition.

23 D Monopolistic competition involves a number of competing producers. A market with one dominant producer is somewhere between oligopoly and monopoly.

24 A There is no differentiation under perfect competition.

25 A A monopsony is a market with a single buyer. This is a definition.

26 C Any unilateral price change brings a disadvantage to the supplier concerned. This is illustrated by a kinked demand curve.

27 D Examples would include some utilities, which usually involve an extensive capital infrastructure.

28 D Monopolies tend to produce at a level below that which offers the lowest average cost and therefore they do not achieve technical efficiency.

29 C The monopolist's demand curve is also the market demand since there are no other producers.

30 C Homogeneity means the producers are in competition with one another.

31 C Predatory pricing is the name sometimes given to the temporary lowering of prices by a monopolist, to deter other firms which might be considering entry into the market, so Statement C is incorrect.

Statement A is correct. By having over-capacity a monopolist can deter would-be rivals from entering the market. This is because it would be able to threaten an increase in output, lower production costs and so lower and more competitive prices.

Statement B is correct. When economies of scale are achievable at high volumes of output, a single firm should be able to monopolise the market by producing most of the market output at a cost (and price) that rivals cannot match.

Statement D is correct. When barriers to **exit** from a market are low, because a firm will suffer few or no sunk costs if it decides to leave the market, the market will become more contestable.

32 B Statement A is correct because it is an example of the same product being sold at two or more different prices, according to the time of day. Statement D is true: the same good or service may be sold at different prices in different geographical areas, to people of different ages (eg half price for children), on the basis of time (eg see Statement A) or because consumers in one market are ignorant of lower prices in another market. Statement C is correct, because price discrimination for a good in two geographical markets can only be sustained if it is too expensive for a customer to buy goods in the low-price market, incur transport costs to ship them to the higher –price market, and sell them at a competitive price in that market. Statement B is incorrect, because production costs should not have any influence on price discrimination, only a firm's output levels.

33	D	First and second class tickets are not an example of price discrimination, because even though they are tickets for the same aeroplane journey, they are different products – eg in terms of service and travel comfort – rather than the same product being sold at two or more different prices. All the other statements are true, with B and C being key conditions for price discrimination to be achievable.
34	B	Costs are irrelevant. Identical PED means identical response to price changes, so proposition (iv) is incorrect.
35	C	Low fixed costs make entry and exit easy.
36	A	Perfect knowledge is one of the assumptions of perfect competition.
37	D	This enables them to control the market and thereby sustain a super-normal profit.
38	B	If a firm makes 1,000 units of output using 10 units of labour and 10 units of capital, say, it is **technically efficient** if a reduction in the amount of labour or capital will mean that the firm cannot make 1,000 units of output any more (ie there is no resource wastage in the current set up). A firm can be technically efficient combining inputs in a number of different ways or mixes to produce a given quantity of output, and so in this example, the firm could produce 1,000 units with a variety of different mixes of labour and capital. If it produces the 1,000 units with the mix that minimises average cost, the firm is **economically efficient.**

Option C (Price equals marginal cost) denotes allocative efficiency.

39	A	It will produce where MC = MR. Since MC will always be positive, this point must be where MR is also positive, ie on the elastic portion of the demand curve. (Technically, the price elasticity of demand will be less than –1, but the convention in economics is to often ignore the minus sign, therefore the number has to be bigger than 1.)
40	D	There are barriers to the entry of competitors. Note that economies of scale (Option B) are not confined to any particular market structure.
41	B	If the long run average costs are constant, then there are no significant economies of scale. The existence of economies of sale is one of the barriers to entry to a monopoly market.
42	B	This will cause a downward shift in the marginal cost curve. A could have resulted in output reaching Q_2 by increasing the demand (shifting AR and therefore MR to the right), but this would have produced a higher price than P_2.
43	D	The marginal cost curve cuts the average total cost curve at its minimum value, So average costs will be minimised at the point where MC = AC.
44	B	In an oligopoly, a small number of firms dominate the market.
45	A	If firms collude, they will act like a monopolist.
46	B	If price discrimination is possible, the monopolist can segment the market. This is likely to *increase* output, and with lower prices being offered to some segments, allocative inefficiency will be reduced.
47	A	Each firm faces a downward sloping demand curve so II is incorrect. Product differentiation is a key aspect of monopolistic competition. Firms only operate at full capacity under perfect competition so I is also true.

48	A	Market concentration

49 C The five firm concentration ratio compares the share of the five largest firms to the industry total. In this case, that is C, D, E, G, and H.

$$17 + 19 + 26 + 18 + 20 = 100$$

$$\frac{100}{143} = 70\%$$

50 D Perfect competition

51 C **Monopolistic competition** is characterised by a large number of producers making extensive use of product differentiation. **Oligopoly** is characterised by interdependence of decision making on price and output between firms.

52 C **Game theory**. Game theory illustrates the problem of interdependent decision-making in the duopoly and oligopoly. It illustrates that firms are better off by working together (colluding) than competing with each other.

53 B CM Co will not be able to raise prices (option A) as being in a perfectly competitive market it is a price taker. Option C (creating barriers to entry) is not possible either in a perfectly competitive market.

Option D increasing production will not work if it is currently making normal profits, because increasing production will mean that MC > MR.

54 D Both A and B are incorrect as with no barriers to entry no single firm or group of firms will be able to acquire the market share for a monopoly or oligopoly.

C is incorrect since with no barriers to entry, firms can enter the market, increase supply, reduce prices and thus prevent higher than normal profits occurring.

55 D A firm's total revenue is maximised when marginal revenue is zero. Note, the question asked for total *revenue*, not *profit*.

If it were to increase output beyond that point, with a downward sloping demand curve, it would have negative marginal revenue for the extra unit of output, meaning that the additional unit has actually decreased its total revenue.

56 C Perfect knowledge is a characteristic of a perfectly competitive market and so is not a barrier to entry. The other three are barriers to entry. High fixed costs are often a characteristic of natural monopolies.

57 C Both oligopolies and monopolistic competition use product differentiation as a means of competing. However, oligopolies have barriers to entry which markets exhibiting monopolistic competition do not. Barriers to entry enable a firm to sustain supernormal profits in the long run.

58 B A characteristic of a contestable market is that entry and exit are relatively easy so firms will leave or join the market depending on the level of profits which are being earned.

Chapter 7

1   D   Regulatory capture involves regulations favouring producers rather than consumers.

2   C   The first three options are arguments in favour of privatisation. The fourth (management of natural monopolies) is an argument in favour of nationalisation.

3   B   The Director General of Fair Trading may ask the Competition Commission to investigate if any firm or group of firms controls 25% or more of the market.

4   C   State owned industries are more likely to respond to the public interest, ahead of the profit motive which underlies privatised industries. This is a reason why key industries (for example, health) may be retained under central control.

5   B   The Private Finance Initiative (PFI) enlists private sector capital and management expertise to provide public services at reduced cost to the public sector budget.

Chapter 8(a)

1   D   Venture capital is a source of funds for start-up companies.

2   A   When building societies offer short-term savings and long-term lending (mortgages) they are providing maturity transformation.

3   A   Financial intermediation is the process of taking deposits from customers and re-lending to borrowers (at a higher rate of interest). Item B could refer to a firm of 'market makers'. Item C refers to a leasing company or finance house. Item D refers to the former role of the discount houses.

4   D   Maturity transformation is a feature of the role of financial intermediaries, such as building societies and banks. Item B describes 'redemption value'. Item C is sometimes described as a yield curve.

5   B   The retail banks primarily take deposits and make loans in the retail market.

6   C   Commercial paper. Commercial paper is a source of finance for banks and companies with good credit ratings.

7   A   Bank overdrafts are arranged between a bank and a specific customer. They cannot be traded separately by financial intermediaries.

8   B   Bank overdraft. A firm must finance long-term investments with long-term financial instruments.

9   D   A long-term project should be financed with long-term finance.

10   D   None of the above. Financial intermediaries do bring together borrowers and lenders.

11   True   Financial intermediaries borrow funds from ultimate lenders and lend it to ultimate borrowers.

12   **Insurance** is concerned with risks that might occur; **assurance** is concerned with risks that will occur.

13   D   All of the above.

14   A   Indirect finance in the flow of funds scheme involves the use of a financial intermediary

15	D	Intermediaries provide the link between people with surplus funds and those needing to borrow.
16	C	The interbank market is the market in which **banks** lend **short-term** funds to one another.
17	C	Financial instruments with maturities of less than one year are traded in the money market.
18	D	Both II and IV. The bond can be sold in a capital market and a secondary market.
19	A	Both I and III. Short term financial instruments are issued in money markets and primary markets. Money markets are used for lending and borrowing largely short-term capital. Capital markets are used for raising and investing largely long-term capital.
20	A	A treasury bill is short-term.
21	D	Preference share.
22	A	The long term interest rate is normally but not always higher than the short-term rate.
23	C	If the market rate of interest rises, the price of bonds will fall. Bonds paying fixed interest become relatively less attractive compared to a variable interest-bearing investment.
24	False	The calendar used in this context has 365 days.
25	True	Only new issues are traded on primary markets.
26	A	Gilts are issued by the government to finance its budget deficit.
27	D	The main difference between government bonds and corporate bonds is their risk. Government bonds are very low risk.
28	B	A **callable** bond allows the issuer to redeem the bond earlier than its maturity date.
29	B	A **convertible** bond allows the conversion of **bonds** into shares.
30	B	**Preference shares** have priority over **ordinary shares**.
31	C	In **cumulative** preference shares if a firm does not distribute dividends in any year, these unpaid dividends are carried forward from year to year.
32	C	The inability to borrow funds directly from savers.
33	B	Indirect finance.
34	A	**Preference shares** and **bonds** pay a fixed amount per year.
35	C	Reinsurance involves an insurance company passing some risk on to another insurer in exchange for part of the premium.
36	B	Building societies.
37	C	To transfer risk.
38	D	In a whole life policy the length of the contract is indefinite; it pays a certain amount on the death of the insured party.
39	A	In a term life policy the length of the contract is fixed.
40	B	Underwriters only deal with primary markets.

41   C   A corporate bond holder receives a fixed payment.

42   C   The four main functions of money are: medium of exchange; store of value; unit of account; and standard of deferred payment.

Chapter 8(b)

1   A   Fiscal policy is about government finance, not bank finance.

2   C   The bank is liable to customers for amounts deposited.

3   D   These are **very** short term deposits. Stocks and shares change value daily. Paintings are highly illiquid.

4   B   This specifically reduces the risk of default.

5   B   The rate of tax paid by the business should not affect the rate charged.

6   C   Banks' retail deposits. Narrow money is defined as M_0; broad money as M_4.

7   B   A is 'the multiplier' in the context of national income. Note this is completely separate from the credit multiplier used in the context of banking.

8   A   A commercial bank must try to balance the three main areas of profitability, liquidity and security.

9   C   Determining the public sector borrowing requirement is a government role.

10   D   Elasticity is not a meaningful concept in this context.

11   C   Setting the rate at which it lends to commercial banks.

12   B   Fiscal policy relates to the government's taxation, borrowing and spending plans. The central bank is not responsible for fiscal policy.

13   C   Customers' deposits are **liabilities** of a bank, not assets. The assets of a typical retail bank include notes and coin (till money), and near-liquid assets such as deposits with money market institutions (eg inter-bank loans), bills of exchange and certificates of deposit (CDs). Most of the assets of a retail bank are their loans and overdrafts to customers.

14   C   If the banks maintained a 10% cash ratio, the credit multiplier for any initial increase in cash deposit will be 1/10% = 10 times.

Maximum increase in bank deposits   = $1 million $\times$ 5 banks $\times$ 10 (credit multiplier)
                                     = $50 million

However, this $50 million includes the initial deposits of $5 million, and so the **further** increase in total bank deposits is $50 million – $5 million = $45 million.

15 B The solution can be shown by algebra. The extra cash deposited with the banks ($C) is already a part of the money supply, and so using the credit multiplier formula, we have:

$$\frac{C}{20\%} = 300 + C$$

C   = 20% (300 + C)
0.8C = 60
C   = 75

If $75 million extra is deposited with banks, the total volume of deposits or cash (ie the money supply) will rise to $75 million ÷ 20% = $375 million. This includes the initial $75 million, and so the money supply will increase by $300 million. (A temptation might have been to give answer A here).

16 False One of the largest liabilities on banks' balance sheets is customers' deposits. The relevant assets in the bank's balance sheet is advances made to customers.

17 False A bank does not keep on hand as reserves all of the money entrusted to its deposits. It only keeps a proportion of them, in line with its reserve ratio.

18 B The actual deposit expansion multiplier will be reduced if individuals hold currency rather than depositing it in a bank.

19 D (iii) and (iv). A central bank purchasing government securities will increase the money supply and increase the monetary base.

20 C If expected inflation is negative, the nominal interest rate is **less** than the real interest rate, and **positive**.

21 A Treasury bill

22 B The running yield of a bond is defined as the ratio of coupon to the market value of the bond.

23 True The redemption yield shows the return for a bond held to maturity.

24 True The yield curve shows the relationship between bond yields of various maturities.

25 C (0.03 + (6.50 − 6))/6 = 8.83%

26 D The yield is a measure of the return from an investment.

27 B If interest rates go up, the required rate of return on equities will go **up** and equity prices will **fall**.

28 C The bond holder will receive 4% of $1,000 = $40. $40 as a percentage of the current market price of $800 is 5%.

29 D The credit multiplier is 1/credit reserve ratio. 1/20% = 5

5 × $100 = $500.

30 B Real rate of interest $= \dfrac{1 + \text{nominal rate}}{1 + \text{inflation rate}} = \dfrac{1.15}{1.06} = 8.5\%$

Chapter 9

1   A   3
      B   4
      C   5
      D   1
      E   2

2   Withdrawals from the circular flow of income are **savings**, **taxation** and **expenditure on imports**.

3   Net property income from abroad.

4   Capital consumption.

5   C   All income received. This is the definition.

6   B   Given that $Y = C + I + G + (X - M)$, to avoid a fall in National Income G must be offset by an increase in C, I (item 3) or X (item 1).

7   A   Net National Product at factor cost plus capital consumption equals Gross National Product at factor cost. By adding back taxes on expenditure and subtracting subsidies, we then get from GNP at factor cost to GNP at market prices.

8   B   Transfer payments are payments where the recipient does not make any contribution to national output in return. They involve the transfer of wealth rather than a reward for creating economic wealth, and a redistributing of income from taxpayers to others. Salaries of Members of Parliament are a part of general government expenditure and so are included in the National Income figures.

9   A   Increasing inventory levels is an investment, because it involves incurring expenditures now for some benefit in the future time. Although the purchase of shares (item B), second hand machinery (item C) or an already-existing company (item D) are all investments for the individuals or organisations concerned, they are merely the transfer of ownership of already-existing assets, and there is no creation of *new* non-current asset capital investment or inventories. From the point of view of the national economy as a whole, these do not count as investment and do not provide an injection into the circular flow.

10 A

	20X3 $ million	20X4 $ million
Consumers' expenditure	200,000	225,000
Government expenditure	70,000	74,000
Fixed capital formation	54,000	60,000
	324,000	359,000
Exports	93,000	94,000
Imports	(92,000)	(99,000)
GDP at market prices	325,000	354,000

Increase (354 – 325)   = $29,000 million

% Increase in money terms   = $\dfrac{29,000}{325,000} \times 100\% = 8.9\%$

% change in real terms, with 10% inflation, is a fall of about 1%

Note: No adjustment is needed for taxes and subsidies because the question asks about GDP at *market prices*

11 D   Capital consumption represents an estimated cost based on **current prices** for the gradual using up of the nation's productive fixed assets. It is difficult to estimate accurately. Statement A is incorrect, largely because inter-country comparisons of living standards would be based on National Income per **head** rather than total National Income. Statement B is incorrect because services provided free such as policing are included in the statistics at actual cost. Statement C is wrong because when there is a strong black economy, with economic activity not reported to the government to avoid taxation, official statistics will **underestimate** National Income.

12 B

	$m
GDP at factor cost	150
Add taxes	17
Less subsidies	−10
GDP at market prices	157

Note. Government expenditure is already included in GDP at factor cost.

Chapter 10

1   Y_2. Y_2 represents full employment level. The vertical aggregate supply curve shows that the economy cannot produce any additional output because its resources are already fully employed.

2   A   It is an inflationary gap.

3   C   Poor households have a higher propensity to consume since they need most of their income to pay for subsistence. Therefore a redistribution of income from rich to poor households is likely to lead to an increase in aggregate demand. Remember the multiplier is: $\dfrac{1}{1-MPC}$

4    $20bn

$$\Delta NI \quad = \frac{\text{Injection}}{1 - MPC}$$

$$= \frac{\$2bn}{1 - 0.9}$$

$$= \$20bn$$

5   False. The accelerator principle helps to explain the existence of the business cycle by showing how investment changes **disproportionately** in response to changes in consumption.

6   D   The relationship between changes in income and changes in consumption.

7   C   Items A and B describe the multiplier effect. Item D is not correct, because although *Keynes* believed that a combination of the multiplier and the accelerator helped to cause trade cycles, this is not the accelerator principle as such. Item C correctly states that if firms have a fixed capital:output ratio, an increase in output will create a bigger proportional increase in investment in new capital equipment, so that more capital goods will be produced.

8   A   Changes in GDP can measure (and so indicate) trade cycle movements. A number of economic indicators show movements in the trade cycle, either rising (eg raw material prices) or falling (eg unemployment, bankruptcies) during a period of expansion, and the opposite during a recession. Seasonal unemployment rises or falls according to the season of the year (eg jobs for cricketers or ski instructors) and changes in this are not indicative of any business cycle movements.

9   D   Remember the multiplier formula! The marginal propensity to import (m) and the marginal rate of taxation (t) help to reduce the size of the multiplier, in addition to the marginal propensity to save (s).

10   A   When an economy booms, it reaches a turning point and goes into recession. The recession deepens into a depression. Eventually, there is another turning point in the economy, and the business cycle goes into recovery and then back into boom, and so on.

11   A   Lower interest rates should be a consequence of an increase in the money supply, with a movement along the liquidity preference curve rather than a shift in the liquidity preference curve (item B).

12   D   Keynes' analysis of inflation considered the situation where aggregate demand exceeded the ability of the economy to produce real output to meet the demand, resulting in demand-pull inflation and an inflationary gap.

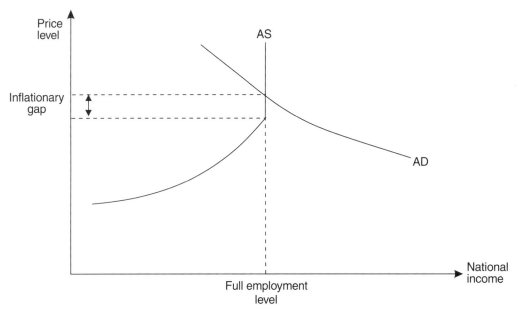

13   False. This is what the accelerator principle does.

14    $10bn

$$\Delta NI \quad = \frac{\Delta J}{1 - MPC}$$

$$= \frac{\$2bn}{1 - 0.8}$$

$$= \$10bn$$

15   B   Keynes argued that an increase in the money supply would lead to lower interest rates while monetarists argue that an increase in the money supply would lead to higher inflation.

16   True.   Aggregate demand will increase by the full amount of government expenditure. At the same time an increase in taxation will reduce disposable income and consumption. However, since the marginal propensity to consume is less than 1, then the fall in consumption will be less than the increase in government expenditure resulting in an increase in output since aggregate demand is higher.

17   A   Recession and declining demand go together. Inflation and declining demand do not. The trade balance is likely to improve due to a decrease in demand for imports.

18   A   A rise in cyclical unemployment is a *consequence* of a fall in the level of economic activity rather than its *cause*

19   A   The marginal propensity to consume plus the marginal propensity to save must equal 1.

20 C The multiplier in an open economy $= \dfrac{1}{s+m+t}$

If taxes are 20%, savings are 10% and domestic consumption is 50%, the balance (imports) must be 20%.

So the multiplier is $\dfrac{1}{0.1+0.2+0.2} = \dfrac{1}{0.5} = 2$

21 A National income needs to rise by $25m, but the multiplier is $\dfrac{1}{1-\text{MPC}} = \dfrac{1}{1-0.8} = 5$.

So the increase needed is $25m/5 = $5m.

Chapter 11

1 Right to left. Stagflation is characterised by a fall in employment and a rise in prices.

2 D Nominal rate of interest = Real rate of interest + Rate of inflation (approx) = 3% + 6% = 9%.

3 A Items B, C and D will all be measures which reduce the demand for goods and services. Public expenditure (item D) represents the government's own demand. Bank lending (item C) is largely used for spending on goods and services by the people who borrow the money. Higher value added tax (item B) could increase total spending on goods and services **inclusive** of the tax, but spending **net** of tax will fall, and this should result in a reduction in demand-pull inflation. Item A, lower interest rates, is likely to result in higher consumer borrowing and even stronger demand-pull inflation.

4 B $690 \times \dfrac{100}{120} = 575$

5 C Structural unemployment is caused by a mismatch between available jobs and the unemployed. This could be caused by a geographical mismatch or by a mismatch of skills. Items B and D could be **causes** of structural unemployment, but don't fully describe it.

6 True. Import cost push inflation occurs when the cost of essential imports rise regardless of whether or not they are in short supply.

7 Structural.

8 C Seasonal unemployment fluctuates in seasonal patterns throughout the year.

9 C Structural unemployment is best tackled by supply side measures. Demand management can only affect demand-deficient (cyclical) unemployment.

10 A = inflation
  B = unemployment

11 NAIRU

12 A deflationary gap represents the extent to which the planned level of aggregate demand will need to shift upwards to reach the full employment level of national income.

13   False. The correct name is **demand pull** inflation.

14   D   This is an example of demand pull inflation.

15   B   Structural unemployment occurs as a result of long-term changes in the conditions of an industry.

16   B   This is a definition of the natural rate hypothesis or the non-accelerating inflation rate of unemployment (NAIRU).

17   A   Friedman argued that stimulating demand will only have a temporary effect on unemployment, and that demand-led expansion of the economy would soon become inflationary (with no increase in the real output). He argued in favour of supply side measures to reduce the natural rate of unemployment. Retraining schemes (item B) should reduce structural unemployment. Cutting trade union power (item C) was seen as a way of reducing unemployment. Lower income taxes (item D) and lower benefits for the unemployed would make individuals more willing to work and less willing to remain unemployed.

18   B   A revaluation of the currency (item A) should make import costs cheaper. An increase in direct taxation (item B) will not reduce pressures for higher costs; if anything, it will encourage workers to demand higher wages, which will add to cost-push inflationary pressures. Wage drift (item C) is the tendency for annual wages increases to run ahead of the rate of inflation and to 'drift' upwards, and controlling this would reduce inflationary pressures from higher costs. Linking wage and salary increases to productivity improvements (item D) will help to keep unit costs down, and so reduce cost-push inflationary pressures.

19   C   Employers' National Insurance contributions are paid by firms to the government for each of their employees. A reduction in these contributions will, in effect, reduce the cost of labour. Lower wages costs will increase the demand for labour by firms. Higher VAT, a higher budget surplus and lower spending on nationalised industries (items A, B and D) would all reduce spending/demand in the economy, and so should be expected to **increase** the level of unemployment.

Chapter 12

1   D   Unemployment and welfare payments.

2   A   The gap between government expenditure and government receipts.

3   A   A budget deficit increases government debt.

4   B   The government debt represents the amount of outstanding gilts the government has issued.

5   D   The number of transactions (T) has to be unchanged for the equation MV = PT to be a predictor of price behaviour. Any increase in M, given no change in V in the short run, would result in a matching percentage increase in prices P.

6   Prices will rise by 5%.

7   A, C   Higher interest rates should **discourage consumer spending** with borrowed money and spending on credit. Higher interest rates should **attract** investors into sterling. They should also discourage

borrowing, and since borrowing from banks and building societies is the main cause of increases in the broad money supply, there should be some **slowing down** of money supply growth.

8   B   Low interest rates will encourage spending rather than saving. Investment will be encouraged because the opportunity cost of investing is reduced.

9   True.   Suppose that the central bank reduces interest rates. With given wages and prices, this is also a reduction in the real interest rate. Lower real interest rates raise investment demand and (autonomous) consumption and hence aggregate demand and equilibrium output.

10   A   A flat-rate tax, with no concession for the lower-paid, would take a higher proportion of the income of lower-income earners than of higher-income earners. Taxes that have this effect are regressive taxes. Television licences and road tax for cars are examples.

11   D   A reduction in taxes on alcoholic drinks will leave all consumers of alcohol with more income. A less even distribution of wealth in society means that richer people will now be relatively better off than before, which means that they have obtained a bigger benefit from the tax cuts. The conclusion points to either answer B or answer D. The benefit has to be **relative**, since the distribution of wealth refers to relative (proportionate) wealth, and so answer D must be correct.

12   C   The opportunity cost of leisure will fall if fewer goods and services can be bought with income earned from working. An **increase** in the rate of tax on income or on goods that can be bought with income will have this effect, and so item C is correct. A flat rate poll tax levied on all individuals, working or not working, does not alter the opportunity cost of working. Similarly, a capital transfer tax does not have a direct bearing on the opportunity cost of working, because it is only applied when individuals transfer wealth to each other, not when income is earned from working.

13   D   Fiscal policy is concerned with the government's tax income, expenditure and borrowing (to make up the difference between income and expenditure).

14   C   It is aggregate supply in the economy which is at issue.

15   D   Higher taxation will tend to reduce consumer spending. Higher import tariffs might result in greater consumer expenditure on imports inclusive of tariffs, but the volume and the net-of-tariff value of imports purchased will fall. Higher social security payments will give consumers more cash to spend.

16   B   The concept of liquidity preference refers to people's preference to hold their savings as money rather than investing them when the rate of return from both is equal.

17   C   If interest rates are low, but expected to rise this implies that bond prices are likely to fall. People will hold funds so that they can invest in bonds later, so liquidity preference is high (option i). If interest rates are low, the speculative demand for money will be high (option iii).

18   B   This question applies the quantity theory of money, MV = PT.

$M \times 4 = \$50 \times 10$ million
So $M = \$(500/4)$ million $= \$125$ million.

19   B   Monetarist economists consider supply side measures the best way to manage the economy, in contrast to Keynesians who prefer fiscal and demand-led policies.

20   A   This is the central argument of monetarist theory.

21 The public sector net cash requirement (PSNCR) is the annual excess of spending over income for the entire public sector (government plus other public authorities).

22 A   Options C & D relate to monetary policy. Fiscal policy looks at levels of government expenditure and how they can be funded through tax revenues.

Chapter 13(a)

1   B   A spot rate is the rate set for the delivery of currency now.

2   B   A forward rate is the rate for delivery of the currency at some future date.

3   B   The Purchasing Power Parity Theory predicts that the exchange value of a currency depends on relative prices.

4   €400,000 being $500,000 × 0.800.

5   C   The current inflation rate in the US is running at 6% and 5% in the UK. The exchange rate between the two countries is 1.78 $/$.

$$\text{Exchange rate in one year's time} = 1.78 \times \frac{1.06}{1.05} = 1.7970$$

6   B   The interest rate parity condition or theory explains the difference between spot and forward exchange rates in terms of the relative interest rates in the two countries.

7   B   Below the spot rate because the UK interest rate is higher.

8   B   The currency risk is maximised.

9   D   Having a single currency need not mean that interest notes are standardised..

10 A   Transaction risk arises when the prices of imports or exports are fixed in foreign currency terms and there is a change in exchange rates between the date the price is agreed and the date when the transaction takes place.

11 A   A rise in US interest rates is likely to prompt a flow of funds from UK to US increasing the relative demand (and value) of the dollar, meaning a corresponding relative fall in the value of sterling.

12 The exchange rate will fall. An increase in supply of anything tends to lead to a fall in its price.

13 True. The country with the higher inflation rate will eventually be forced to devalue.

14 B   A marked deterioration in the UK's balance of trade is likely to lead to a **decrease** in the value of sterling. There will be **increased** need to buy foreign currency to pay for imports. (Demand for foreign currency will go up, demand for sterling will go down.)

15 B   A and D are benefits of fixed exchange rates; C does not apply to any exchange rate system.

16 C   It sometimes seems that *anything* can contribute to pressure on fixed exchange rates, but changes in unemployment are unlikely to do so. A case might be made for suggesting that falling unemployment might herald cost push inflation which might in turn put downward pressure on an exchange rate, but this is unlikely.

17   D   A single currency requires a single monetary policy.

18   A   B and D are characteristic of fixed exchange rates. C can only happen with a common currency; however, a fixed exchange rate can eliminate the costs associated with managing exchange rate risk, such as the cost of hedging.

19   True.

20   B   Member nations retain control over fiscal policy, though there are limitations on their freedom of action.

21   C   The sum of the balance of payments accounts must always balance (to zero). A surplus on the current account will be matched by a deficit on the financial and capital accounts, and vice versa.

22   D   Devaluation of the currency will make imports more expensive. The price of exports should not be directly affected by the devaluation, and so the terms of trade (unit value of exports ÷ unit value of imports) will worsen. Higher costs of imports will add to the cost of living.

23   D   Exchange rates in the foreign exchange markets are determined by the interaction of demand and supply. An excessive outflow of sterling from the UK means either that there are large capital outflows or that there are large outflows caused by a balance of payments deficit. This will create an extra supply of sterling for sale in the foreign exchange markets, and the price of sterling, which is the exchange rate for sterling against other traded currencies, would fall.

24   C   With a depreciation in the value of sterling, import prices rise, because it costs more in $ sterling to obtain the foreign currency to pay foreign suppliers for the imported goods. Since demand for imports is inelastic, the fall in demand for imports resulting from an increase in their price will be relatively small, and total spending on imports will rise.

25   C   When a currency appreciates in value, imports become cheaper to buy but exports become more expensive for foreign buyers. Demand for imports is price inelastic, and so a fall in the price of imports will result in a fall in total spending on imports. Exports prices in Gerdaland's own currency will be unchanged, but prices to foreign buyers will go up. Higher export prices to foreign buyers will result in a fall in total export volumes and so in total export revenue for Gerdaland.

26   D   Higher interest rates should attract more investments from abroad into the country and so there will be **capital inflows** into the country. The capital inflows should cause an **appreciation in the currency**, because foreign investors must buy the currency to pay for their investments in the country. With an appreciation in the currency, imports become cheaper to buy and exports become more expensive to foreign buyers. With inelastic demand, this means that total spending on imports will fall. The volume of exports will fall, and so total revenue from exports in the exporter's **domestic current domestic currency** will fall too. (Total spending by foreign buyers on exports will rise, but only in their own currency.)

Chapter 13(b)

1   False. This describes **absolute** advantage.

2   Guns. It has to give up 15 tons of butter to produce one gun domestically, but it can obtain one from Country X in exchange for only 10 tons of butter. Country Y has the comparative advantage in producing butter. It should concentrate on producing butter and import guns from country X.

3   False. 'Dumping' is exporting goods at less than a fair cost in order to support domestic industry.

4   False. This may be useful but it is not essential.

5   A   B, C and D all apply.

6   D   A rise in interest rates will enlarge a *deficit* on the balance of trade. The rise in interest rates will lead to a *rise* in the exchange rate. This will make exports *more expensive* and imports *cheaper*, thus causing the balance of trade to deteriorate.

7   A   Current account balance
      B   Time

8   C   Opportunity cost is the key to understanding comparative advantage.

9   D   Tariffs allow domestic producers to raise their prices which would generate cost-push inflation.

10   B   The theory is founded on opportunity cost.

11   D   This statement is nonsense.

12   A   The expenditure to be reduced in this context is expenditure on imports. A will tend to do this by deflating the economy.

13   C   D is likely to follow after C.

14   B   This is the only one likely to boost import demand.

15   C   Reduced exchange rate uncertainty, and increased price transparency are two of the benefits of joining a single currency.

16   C   The terms of trade relate import and export **prices**.

17   B   Financing a deficit requires **foreign** currency.

18   A   This would apply to **all** goods, whether imported or not.

19   D   Note that the question asks about **capital** markets.

20   A   This is a problem for government management of international trade and the balance of payments for its country alone.

21   D   Supply and demand are inelastic. A point of definition, known as the Marshall-Lerner condition.

22   B   This will tend to increase the unit value of exports. Note that the terms of trade relate to the *price* of exports to the price of imports, rather than the relative volume of exports and imports.

23   C   Country X has an **absolute** advantage over Country Y in making P and Q, because 1 unit of resource in Country X will make more of either P or Q than one unit of resource in Country Y. However, international trade should still take place because of **comparative** advantage in producing P and Q.

The opportunity costs of producing a unit of P is $(^4/_8) = {}^1/_2$ unit of Q in Country X and only $^1/_3$ unit of Q in Country Y.

Similarly, the opportunity cost of producing a unit of Q is 2 units of P in Country X and 3 units of P in Country Y.

Country X has a comparative advantage in producing P and Country Y has a comparative advantage in the production of Q. International trade should be beneficial for both countries, with Country X exporting P and Country Y exporting Q.

24   False. The J curve effect is a short run phenomenon.

25   D   Globalisation by definition would see a reduced independence of national economies.

26   False. Volumes of imports and exports must also be considered in the *balance* of trade (as distinct from the *terms* of trade).

27   C   The Marshall-Lerner condition states that in order for a reduction in the exchange rate to bring about an improvement in a country's balance of payments, the sum of the price elasticities of demand and supply must be greater than 1.

28   180

$$\frac{20X6 \text{ exports index}/20X5 \text{ exports index}}{20X6 \text{ imports index}/20X5 \text{ imports index}} = 0.8$$

$$\frac{144/150}{216/x} = 0.8$$

$$144/150 = 0.8 \left(\frac{216}{x}\right)$$

$$\frac{144/150}{0.8} = \frac{216}{x}$$

$$x = \frac{216 \times 0.8}{144/150}$$

$$= 180$$

29   True. The **terms** of trade look at the relationship between export and import prices. The **balance** of payments also depends on changes in the **volume** of exports and imports which will be affected by elasticity.

30   A   To Bandia, the opportunity cost of producing 1 tonne of rice is $^1/_{15}$ car and the opportunity cost of making a car is 15 tonnes of rice.

To Sparta, the opportunity cost of producing rice is higher than in Bandia, because it is $^1/_6$ car. the opportunity cost of making a car is less, because it is just 6 tonnes of rice.

Since Bandia has a comparative advantage over Sparta in producing rice and Sparta has a comparative advantage over Bandia in making cars, international trade will occur, with Bandia exporting rice and Sparta exporting cars.

31   C

	Unit value of exports		Unit value of imports					Terms of trade
Base year	100	÷	100	×	100	=		100
Current level	108	÷	120	×	100	=		90

32   A   The terms of trade are not an item in the Balance of Payments figures. All the other items represent capital movements between the UK and abroad, and would be reported as increases or decreases in UK external assets and liabilities.

33   C   The balance of payments current account is in deficit when there is a deficit on the combined visible and invisible balance. Capital movements are not included, and so item 2 is irrelevant. The invisible balance includes services such as **tourism** (item 1). British tourism abroad creates an outflow and has an adverse effect on the balance of payments. **Transfers** as an item of invisible trade includes such items as payments by the UK government to the European community and the United Nations, and cash grants to developing countries (item 3).

34   C   If real incomes rise in the UK, spending in the UK economy would rise. Some of this extra spending would be on imports.

35   B   'Balance of payments' in the question refers to balance of payment on current account. Capital movements (Reason 2) do **not** have a short-term effect on the balance of payments, although in the longer term, there will be outflows of interest and dividend payments to the foreign investors.

When an economy is reflated, the government will take steps to increase aggregate demand. Some of this extra demand will be satisfied by imported goods (Reason 3) and some by domestically-produced goods. Unless industry has sufficient spare capacity to meet the extra domestic demand and also to carry on producing for the same volume of exports as before, the growth in domestic demand will result in some switch by firms from selling to export market to selling to domestic markets (Reason 1).

36   C   A conclusion from the law of comparative advantage is that if free trade is allowed, countries will specialise in the production of goods and services in which they have a comparative advantage over other countries. As a result, the world's economic resources will be put to their most productive uses, and total output will be maximised. It does not follow that each country of the world will maximise its own National Income of economic wealth (Statement A), because the distribution of the wealth between the individual countries in the world could be uneven, with some countries earning much more than others from their output and their exports.

37   D   In both countries, the opportunity cost of producing wheat is $1/3$ unit of beef, and the opportunity cost of producing beef is 3 units of wheat. Since neither country therefore has a comparative advantage over the other in producing wheat or beef, neither can benefit economically from international trade.

38   D   The balance of **trade** refers to the export and import of visible goods, and does **not** refer to invisible items such as tourism and services. Only item 3, which consists of both imports and exports of visible items, would be included in the balance of trade figures.

39   C   This is just one example of how a country's terms of trade might improve. By switching from low-priced to high-priced products in a major export industry unit export prices will go up and the terms of trade will improve. The change in the **balance** of trade depends on changes in the **volume** of exports and imports **as well as change in export and import prices.**

40   C   Investment in the UK by foreign firms is a capital transaction and does not affect the balance of payments on current account. items A, B and D are all items that will be included in the invisible section of the current account.

41   D   **Reason 1**. with domestic inflation, export prices will go up. Total exports in value might go up or down, depending on the price elasticity of demand for exports. However, higher export prices would improve the terms of trade, not weaken them.

       Reason 2. High prices for domestically produced goods will increase demand for (substitute) imported goods, and so add to total imports.

       Reason 3. If inflation is caused by excess demand in domestic markets, firms will produce goods for their domestic market, and not have the output capacity to export as well. We might say that output has been 'diverted' from export markets to domestic markets, so that total exports will fall in value.

42   D   This is a definition question. An economic and monetary union has a single currency; a common market does not.

43   D   The price of exports will have risen relative to the price of imports, but (a) the balance of payments on current account might either improve or worsen, depending on the price elasticities of demand for exports and imports (b) the exchange rate is dependent on supply and demand for the currency, arising from capital movements and the balance of payments – and is not dependent on changes in the terms of trade, and (c) the terms of trade can improve **either** when export prices go up **or** when import prices fall, and so an improvement in the terms of trade is not **necessarily** a consequence of higher export prices.

44   D   **Consequence 3**. Depreciation of the currency will make imports more expensive. For a country with high imports relative to the size of its national Income, this is likely to lead to some import-cost-push inflation.

       Consequence 2. If demand for imports is inelastic, the increase in import prices will result in an increase in total spending on imports. Exports will be cheaper to foreign buyers, and even if demand is inelastic, total exports will rise in volume and in value. However, with imports increasing and exports increase by only a little, the balance of trade will worsen.

       Consequence 1. with imports prices rising after the depreciation, the terms of trade will **worsen.**

45   B   The balance on the current account is made up of:

	$m
Trade in goods (net position of exports minus imports)	−400
Trade in services (net position of exports minus imports)	250
Income *from* capital investment overseas	150
Transfers *to* overseas bodies	−125
Total	−125

Mock assessments

CIMA

Paper C4 (Certificate)

Fundamentals of Business Economics

Mock Assessment 1

Question Paper	
Time allowed	2 hours
Answer ALL seventy-five questions	

DO NOT OPEN THIS PAPER UNTIL YOU ARE READY TO START UNDER EXAMINATION CONDITIONS

Answer ALL questions

1   In all economies, the best definition of the fundamental economic problem is that:

     A   Consumers never have as much money as they would wish

     B   Resources are scarce relative to human wants

     C   There is always some unemployment of resources

     D   Resources are not always allocated efficiently

2   In economics, which ONE of the following is NOT a cost of production for a firm?

     A   Salaries of senior managers

     B   Normal profit

     C   Interest payable on loans

     D   Corporation tax

3   If the demand for a good is *price inelastic,* then the total expenditure on the good:

     A   Will fall if the price rises

     B   Will be constant if the price rises

     C   Will rise if the price rises

     D   Will rise if the price falls

4   In 20X7, a company made $200m profit from operations, before interest charges of $10m and tax liabilies of $55m.

     Its capital employed was $800m.

     What was the company's retained on capital employed (ROCE)?

     A   16.9%

     B   18.1%

     C   23.8%

     D   25.0%

5   A profit-maximising firm will attempt to produce where:

     A   Marginal cost is equal to marginal revenue

     B   Average costs of production are lowest

     C   Marginal cost equals average cost

     D   Marginal cost is equal to average revenue

6   Which ONE of the following is an example of price discrimination?

    A   A bus company charging a lower price than a railway company for the same distance travelled

    B   A telecommunications company charging reduced rates for telephone calls made in the evening compared to during the day.

    C   Supermarkets charging different prices for fruit in different regions because local supply costs vary

    D   Petrol stations charging lower prices for unleaded petrol than for leaded petrol

7   All of the following are characteristics of oligopolies EXCEPT which ONE?

    A   There is a small number of firms in the industry
    B   There is a preference for non-price competition
    C   There is very little product differentiation
    D   There are entry barriers to the industry

8   Monopolies are undesirable because they:

    A   Control most of the market
    B   Maximise profits
    C   Do not pass on to consumers the benefits of economies of scale
    D   Do not produce where average costs are lowest

9   Which of the following is not a source of funds for capital investment by a business?

    A   Commercial banks
    B   Retained profits
    C   Stock markets
    D   Central bank

10   Which of the following are features of a good corporate governance model?

    (i)   An appropriate balance of executive and non-executive directors
    (ii)   Ensuring the principles of openness, integrity and accountability are adopted
    (iii)   Establish a clear division of responsibilities between the chairman and the chief executive

    A   (i) and (ii)
    B   (i) and (iii)
    C   (ii) and (iii)
    D   All of them

11   Which of the following are functions of money?

(i)   A medium of exchange
(ii)   A store of value
(iii)   A unit of account
(iv)   A measure of liquidity

A   (i) and (ii) only
B   (i), (ii) and (iii) only
C   (ii), (iii) and (iv) only
D   All of them

12   Which ONE of the following is a transfer payment in national income accounting?

A   Educational scholarships
B   Salaries of lecturers
C   Payments for textbooks
D   Payments of examination entry fees

13   Which of the following would increase the potential benefits from international trade?

(i)   The existence of economies of scale in production
(ii)   A high mobility of capital and labour between economies
(iii)   Large differences in the opportunity costs of production between countries
(iv)   Low international transport costs

A   (i), (ii) and (iii) only
B   (ii), (iii) and (iv) only
C   (i), (iii) and (iv) only
D   All of them

14   All of the following would raise the demand for imports in a country except which one?

A   A rise in consumer incomes
B   A reduction in tariffs
C   A rise in the domestic price level
D   A devaluation of the exchange rate

15 Consider the supply of yachts. Just recently, the price of sailcloth used in making sails for yachts has fallen substantially. The supply of yachts is perfectly inelastic in the short term. What would happen in the short term?

A The equilibrium supply quantity and price of yachts would be unchanged

B The supply curve for yachts would shift to the right, and the price of sailing yachts would fall. More yachts would be made and sold

C The supply curve for yachts would shift to the right, and the price of sailing yachts would fall. The same quantity of yachts as before would be made and sold.

D The supply curve for yachts would be unchanged, and the quantity made would be the same as before. However, their price would fall, with cost savings being passed on to the customer

16 Holden Tite is a professional footballer, playing in goal for his team. He earns a wage which is more than sufficient to keep him in his job, and the excess income he earns is called:

A Opportunity cost
B Economic rent
C Transfer earnings
D Surplus value

17 Which of the following statement is *not* true about the price mechanism?

A Monopoly and other restrictive practices obstruct the smooth re-allocation of resources
B In a private enterprise system, the sovereignty of the consumer is complete
C Immobility of factors makes the price mechanism less efficient as an allocative device
D High profits will generally attract resources from less remunerative activities

18 The multiplier effect of government investment is likely to be greater where:

A There is excess production capacity in the private sector of industry
B There is a high marginal propensity to consume
C The increased spending is financed by higher taxation
D There is a high level of inventories in firms

19 According to the view represented by a Phillips curve, which of the following is correct?

A Higher inflation causes unemployment
B Higher unemployment causes inflation
C Unemployment and inflation are not related
D Full employment and low inflation cannot be achieved together

20 The total yield from an indirect tax levied on a good is likely to be greatest when:

A Demand is inelastic, supply is elastic
B Demand is inelastic, supply is inelastic
C Demand is elastic, supply is elastic
D Demand is elastic, supply is inelastic

21   Product T has inelastic demand. The recent introduction of productivity-improving equipment in the manufacture of product T is expected to result, short term, in conditions of excess supply. Which of the following changes is most likely to remove the conditions of excess supply?

A   A fall in price that stimulates a large increase in demand

B   A small reduction in price, resulting in a large shift to the left in the supply curve, and so a large fall in demand

C   A large number of firms will leave the industry, and so total supply will fall

D   A large fall in price, creating a fairly small increase in demand and a large fall in supply

22   Which of the following may cause an increase in National Income?

A   A fall in investment
B   A rise in exports
C   An increase in saving
D   A fall in consumer spending

23   A country's economy is experiencing a low rate of economic growth and a high level of technological unemployment, a form of structural unemployment. A policy by the government aimed at increasing aggregate demand to raise the rate of growth in National Income would have all of the following effects *except* which *one*?

A   It would be inflationary
B   It would create supply bottlenecks
C   It would worsen the balance of trade
D   It would reduce unemployment

24   Which of the following measures can help to tackle the problem of cost-push inflation?

1   Higher direct taxation
2   Wage increases being linked to productivity improvements
3   Higher interest rates
4   A revaluation of the currency

A   Measures 1, 2 and 3 only
B   Measures 1, 2 and 4 only
C   Measures 2, 3 and 4 only
D   Measures 2 and 4 only

25

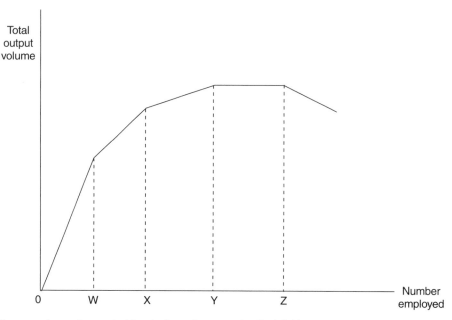

In the diagram above, from what level of employment do diminishing returns start to occur?

A   Above employment level W
B   Above employment level X
C   Above employment level Y
D   Above employment level Z

26   Much Wapping is a small town in Hampshire where a municipal swimming pool and sports centre has just been built by a private firm Bumpsydaisy Co. Which of the following is an external benefit of the project?

A   The increased trade of local shops
B   The increased traffic in the neighbourhood
C   The increased profits for the sports firm
D   The increased building on previously open land

27   International trade is best explained by the fact that:

A   All countries have an absolute advantage in the production of something
B   All countries have specialised in the production of certain goods and services
C   No country has an absolute advantage in the production of all goods and services
D   All countries have a comparative advantage in the production of something

28   All of the following will encourage the process of the globalisation of production except which one?

A   Reductions in international transport costs
B   Higher levels of tariffs
C   Reduced barriers to international capital movements
D   Increased similarity in demand patterns between countries

29   Which one of the following is not one of the three motives which Keynes identified as reasons why people hold money?

A   To pay for day-to-day purchases
B   Because they are crowded out of the banking market
C   As a precaution in case they need it suddenly
D   To be able to take advantage of a profitable opportunity to invest

30   Which ONE of the following shows the lowest degree of international mobility?

A   Unskilled labour
B   Financial capital
C   Technical knowledge
D   Management

31   A deficit on a country's balance of payments current account can be financed by a surplus:

A   Of exports over imports
B   Of invisible exports over invisible imports
C   On the capital account
D   Of taxes over expenditure

32   A fall in the exchange rate for a country's currency will improve the balance of payments current account if:

A   The price elasticity of demand for imports is greater than for exports
B   The price elasticity of demand for exports is greater than for imports
C   The sum of the price elasticities for imports and exports is less than one
D   The sum of the price elasticities for imports and exports is greater than one

33   All of the following are benefits which all countries will gain from the adoption of a single currency such as the euro, except which one?

A   Reduced transactions costs
B   Increased price transparency
C   Lower interest rates
D   Reduced exchange rate uncertainty

34   Compared to a fixed exchange rate system, an economy will benefit from a flexible exchange rate system because:

A   It enables businesses to vary their export prices
B   The government will not have to deflate the economy when balance of payments deficits occur
C   It reduces the cost of acquiring foreign exchange
D   It ensures that businesses never become uncompetitive in international markets

35   What determines the opportunity cost of holding money?

A   The rate of growth in the money supply
B   The rate of price inflation
C   The interest rate on deposits
D   The level of economic output

36   Which *one* of the following would be likely to lead to a fall in the value of the UK pound sterling against the euro?

A   A rise in UK interest rates
B   A rise in interest rates in the Euro Zone
C   The UK central bank buying sterling in exchange for euros
D   Increased capital flows from the Euro Zone to the UK

37   Which of the following would *not* shift the production possibility frontier to the right?

A   An increase in the amount of capital equipment available
B   Introduction of new technology which makes production more efficient
C   An increase in the working population in the economy
D   A fall in unemployment

38   The government has increased government spending without an increase in taxation. Which one of the following is *not* correct?

A   The initial increase in government spending may lead to a larger increase in national income
B   The government is pursuing an expansionary fiscal policy
C   The government's budget deficit will decrease
D   The aggregate demand curve will shift to the right

39   A good has price elasticity of demand of 0.4. Which of the following statements is true?

A   Total consumer expenditure on the good will fall as price rises
B   Total consumer expenditure on the good will rise as price rises
C   Total consumer expenditure on the good will stay the same regardless of any price changes
D   Total consumer expenditure on the good will rise as price falls

↑ supply (selling) → ↓ decrease value £ → ↑ demand foreign currency

40 The diagram below illustrates the effect of a subsidy on the supplier and consumer of a good. The total amount of the subsidy is the distance AB. Which part of this is received by the consumer of the good?

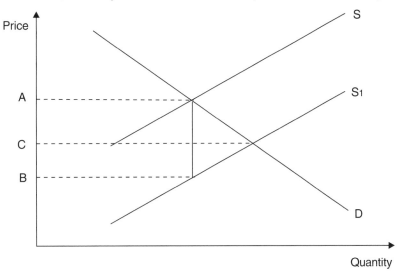

A   AC
B   CB
C   AB
D   None

---

41 If a profit-maximising firm finds that its marginal revenue exceeds its marginal cost, the firm should

A   Increase output no matter whether the firm is a price taker or a price searcher
B   Decrease output no matter whether the firm is a price taker or a price searcher
C   Increase output if the firm is a price taker but not necessarily if the firm is a price searcher
D   Increase output if the firm is a price searcher but not necessarily if the firm is a price taker

---

42 Which of the following accurately states the difference between accounting profit and economic profit?

A   Accounting profit understates economic profit as it includes all expenses including such items as depreciation, amortisation and interest expense

B   Accounting profit understates economic profit, as it includes explicit and implicit costs whereas economic profit considers only explicit cost

C   Accounting profit overstates economic profit, as no allowance is made for the implicit cost of equity capital

D   Accounting profit and economic profit are equal. Both are calculated by subtracting total cost from total revenues

---

43   Which of the following statements is least likely to be true about automatic stabilisers and their role in fiscal policy?

   A   Progressive income taxes, corporate taxes and unemployment compensation are automatic stabilisers

   B   They are forms of countercyclical fiscal policy because they tend to lead to an expansion of the budget deficit in recessionary times and a reduction in the budget deficit in boom times

   C   They implement countercyclical fiscal policy without the problem of time lags associated with discretionary fiscal policy

   D   They require a change in fiscal policy to be effective

44   If a change in price from $10 to $11 causes demand for a good to decrease from 10,000 units to 9,500 units, the arc price elasticity of demand is:

   A   −0.50
   B   −0.54
   C   +0.50
   D   +0.54

45   If the exchange rate for Japanese yen against the US dollar has moved from 110 to 120, then the yen has

   A   Depreciated and US customers will find Japanese goods more expensive
   B   Depreciated and US customers will find Japanese goods cheaper
   C   Appreciated and US customers will find Japanese goods more expensive
   D   Appreciated and US customers will find Japanese goods cheaper

46   Which of the following statements must be true if a firm's average total costs are the same as its average variable costs?

   A   Marginal costs are zero
   B   The firm has achieved technical efficiency
   C   Fixed costs are zero
   D   The firm is producing zero output

47   Which of these statements is least likely to be true?

   A   The short run marginal cost curve cuts both the short run average variable cost curve and the short run average total cost curve at their minimum points

   B   The long run average total cost curve is the envelope of all the short run possibilities

   C   There is one plant size that can produce at all points on the long run average total cost curve

   D   The long run average total cost suggests that as plant size increases, a firm is initially able to benefit from economies of scale

48   When an economy is operating below its full employment level, Keynesian economics is most likely to call for

A   Expansionary fiscal policy
B   Restrictive fiscal policy
C   Expansionary monetary policy
D   Restrictive monetary policy

49   Which of the following would *most likely* be a way of the central bank increasing money supply?

A   Increasing reserve requirements
B   Selling Treasury bonds in the marketplace
C   Issuing Treasury bonds to the marketplace
D   Decreasing the discount rate

50   The cost of producing goods in the US and Germany is as follows.

	US	Germany
	$	$
CD players	50	90
Televisions	60	55

comparative advantage

Which of the following will tend to be correct?

A   Germany will import both CD players and televisions
B   The US will import both CD players and televisions
C   Germany will import CD players and export televisions
D   The US will import CD players and export televisions

51   The crowding out effect caused by an increase in government spending is likely to reduce aggregate demand because

A   Increased government spending causes increases in taxes, reducing aggregate demand

B   Increased government spending causes increases in government borrowing, increasing interest rates and reducing private investment and aggregate demand

C   Increased government spending causes increases in government borrowing, reducing money supply and hence reducing aggregate demand

D   Increased government spending causes increases in government borrowing and taxes, leading to higher savings and lower consumption, thus reducing aggregate demand

52   Which of the following is the best description of the forward rate between two currencies?

A   It reflects market expectations of how the spot rate will move
B   It reflects actual inflation rate differentials between the two currencies
C   It reflects interest rate differentials between the two currencies
D   It is determined by the central banks of the countries concerned

53   The original Phillips curve indicated that there is:

    A   An inverse relationship between the rate of inflation and the level of unemployment
    B   An inverse relationship between the level of unemployment and the money supply
    C   A direct relationship between the rate of inflation and the level of unemployment
    D   A direct relationship between the level of unemployment and the money supply

54   At a price of $80 only, good X has a unitary price elasticity of demand. The demand curve is a straight line. Which of the following is true given a rise in price to $85?

    A   The revenue will remain unchanged
    B   The revenue will increase
    C   The revenue will decrease
    D   Cannot determine the effect in revenue from the information provided

55   All of the following are reasons why the demand curve for a resource may shift, except

    A   A change in the price of the resource
    B   A change in the productivity of the resource
    C   A change in the price of substitute resources
    D   A change in the demand for a product that uses the resource in its production process

56   A firm is considering an investment of $10m.

It applies an interest rate of 10% when discounting future cash flows.

It expects the investment project to yield cashflows of $3m in year 1, $4m in year 2 and $5m in year 3.

Discount rates are 0.909 (year 1), 0.826 (year 2) and 0.751(year 3).

What is the expected net present value of the investment project?

    A $0.91m loss
    B $0.21m loss
    C $0.09 loss
    D $0.21m profit

57   The following graph relates to a monopoly.

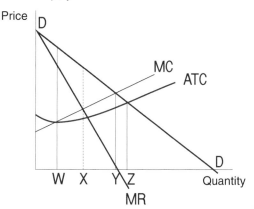

At what quantity would the firm produce?

A   Point W
B   Point X
C   Point Y
D   Point Z

---

58   Which of the following would be a barrier to collusion for an oligopoly?

A   Small number of firms
B   High barriers to entry
C   Antitrust action
D   Cross shareholdings between companies

---

59   In a competitive market where marginal cost intersects average total cost at a point below marginal revenue for an individual firm,

A   Companies are making supernormal profits
B   Companies will shut down production, temporarily or permanently
C   The market is in permanent disequilibrium
D   The demand curve for the industry will shift downwards

---

60   Which of the following is most likely to accompany a fall in the market price of fixed interest bonds?

A   An increase in interest rates
B   A decrease in interest rates
C   An increase in the exchange rate
D   A decrease in the exchange rate

---

61   The spot rate is 0.950-0.965 euro to $1. The three-month forward rate is 0.020-0.035. At what rate would the bank sell euro three-month forward?

A   0.970
B   0.930
C   0.985
D   1.000

hen the price elasticity of demand is inelastic

    Price and total revenue move in the same direction
J   Price and total revenue move in the opposite direction
C   Total revenue increases whether price goes up or down
D   Total revenue remains constant whether price moves up or down

63   The following chart illustrates the domestic prices of three items of similar quality in the United States and Britain.

Items	United States ($)	Britain (£)
Shoes	20	80
Watches	40	180
Electric motors	80	600

If $1 exchanges for £5 and transportation costs and tariffs are zero, Britain will import

A   All three goods from the United States
B   Electric motors and the United States will import shoes and watches
C   Shoes and watches and the United States will import electric motors
D   Import shoes and the United States will import watches and electric motors

64   A Japanese automobile manufacturer builds an automobile plant in the United States. In the foreign exchange market, this action creates

A   A supply of both dollars and yen
B   A demand for both dollars and yen
C   A supply of dollars and a demand for yen
D   A demand for dollars and a supply of yen

65   All of the following are expected impacts of a country's unanticipated shift to a more expansionary monetary policy **except**

A   Real interest rates should rise
B   There will likely be a net capital outflow
C   Value of the domestic currency should depreciate
D   The current account should shift toward a surplus

66   Consider the following statements

(i)   The currency with the lower interest rate will be at a premium in the forward market
(ii)   Forward rates in the currency market reflect an expectation of what the spot rate will be in the future

Which of the following is likely to be correct?

A   Neither statement is true
B   Both statements are true
C   Only statement (i) is true
D   Only statement (ii) is true

67   Which of the following best describes how inflation-indexed bonds can protect investors from inflation and maturity risk?

   A   Inflation-indexed bonds have a floating coupon and a fixed principal

   B   Inflation-indexed bonds have a floating coupon that is linked to interest rates

   C   Inflation-indexed bonds have a principal amount that changes with inflation and a fixed percentage coupon

   D   Inflation-indexed bonds have a principal amount that changes with inflation and a floating percentage coupon

68   The spot rate for the dollar and sterling is $1.6 to £1. Three-month interest rates are 8% for sterling and 6% for dollars. The three-month forward rate is closest to

   A   1.5704
   B   1.6302
   C   1.5922
   D   1.6079

69   Suppose that the central bank raises short term interest rates. What would typically happen to equity prices?

   A   Remain unchanged
   B   Increase
   C   Decrease
   D   Cannot tell

70   When inflation in a country increases relative to the rest of the world, the exchange rate will typically

   A   Fall
   B   Remain unchanged
   C   Rise
   D   Cannot tell

71   Investors in shares of XYZ Co expect to receive a constant dividend payment of $2 per share. If the required rate of return is increased from 8% to 10% the value of the shares will fall by

   A   5%
   B   10%
   C   15%
   D   20%

72   What are the 3E's which are used to assess the performance of public sector and non-profit organisations?

(i)   Earnings
(ii)   Economy
(iii) Effectiveness
(iv)   Efficiency

A   (i), (ii), (iii)
B   (i), (ii), (iv)
C   (i), (iii), (iv)
D   (ii), (iii), (iv)

73   The 'crowding out' effect leads to a fall in:

A   Public spending
B   Private investment
C   Interest rates
D   Export demand

74   The 'J-curve effect' refers to:

A   A firm's experience of initially falling short-run average cost followed by rising average costs

B   The tendency or the marginal propensity to consume to fall as national income rises

C   The tendency of interest rates to vary according to the length of the loan

D   The tendency for balance of payments deficits to deepen before improving following a fall in the exchange rate

75   The 'J-curve effect' is caused by:

A   Inelastic supply
B   Excess demand
C   Capital flows
D   Incomplete recording

Answers

DO NOT TURN THIS PAGE UNTIL YOU HAVE
COMPLETED MOCK ASSESSMENT 1

1   B   Resources are scarce relative to human wants, and this relative scarcity restricts output.

2   D   Tax depends upon tax computations, not economic reality. Don't forget that normal profit is the opportunity cost of enterprise.

3   C   A and D = elastic demand, B = unit elasticity.

4   D $ROCE = \dfrac{PBIT}{Capital\,employed} = \dfrac{\$200m}{\$800m} = 0.25$

5   A   This is a point of definition.

6   B   A relates to two different firms and D relates to two different products. C is tempting, but is wrong because it is the different conditions of supply which lead to the price difference.

7   C   Product differentiation is an important example of non-price competition.

8   D   A and B are not **in themselves** undesirable. C is a political point rather than an economic one.

9   D   A central bank will not provide funds for an individual company.

10 D   These are all features of good corporate governance, as endorsed by the Cadbury Report and the Stock Exchange Combined Code in the UK.

11 B   Different types of money have differing degrees of liquidity.

12 A   A transfer payment is one where no productive service is provided in return for the payment.

13 C   Highly mobile capital and labour could themselves move to wherever they were most efficiently employed and could do this independently of international trade.

14 D   This would make imports more expensive.

15 A   In the short term, supply is perfectly inelastic and so the same quantity of yachts will be made and sold. Given no change in demand conditions, the price will be unchanged too.

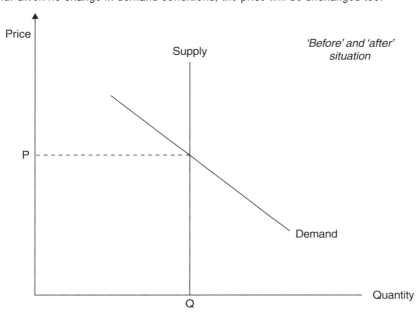

16	B	Economic rent is the surplus of actual earnings for a factor of production over what it could earn in its next best employment.
17	B	'The consumer is king' only when there are perfect markets and perfect competition. With monopoly, monopolistic competition, oligopoly and imperfect markets, the price mechanism still operates but firms wield some influence and the sovereignty of the consumer is not complete.
18	B	The government investment multiplier will work through to private sector investment (through the government multiplier effect). Excess production capacity in industry (item A) and a high level of inventories (item D), however, will avoid the need for **new** investment by industry. A higher rate of marginal taxation (implied by item C) will reduce the multiplier. A high marginal propensity to consume (item B) helps to keep the multiplier high.
19	D	A Phillips curve shows how lower unemployment can only be achieved in conjunction with higher rates of inflation.
20	B	The total yield from an indirect tax is likely to be greatest when (a) demand for the good is relatively unaffected by the addition of a tax on to the price and (b) supply is relatively unaffected, even though suppliers will be receiving the price net of the tax.
21	D	Demand for goods is inelastic and so large changes in demand will not happen; thus, A and B cannot be correct. Event C **might** occur, but the reasons why this should be so are not explained. Event D seems the most likely outcome: a large fall in price will be needed to remove excess supply, and this would also cause a small increase in demand.
22	B	Since $Y = C + I + G + (X - M)$, a fall in C or I would reduce National Income, but a rise in exports X would increase National Income. Savings are a withdrawal from the circular flow and so would reduce national Income, unless they could be diverted into higher investment.
23	D	Technological unemployment is a form of structural unemployment that occurs when people are put out of work by technological developments, possibly because they do not have the necessary skills to work with the new technology. If the government took measures to increase aggregate demand in the economy, domestic firms would be unable to take on more workers to produce more output, because they would be unable to obtain workers with the needed skills, **unless** they spent money on retraining programmes. The expansion in demand would therefore be inflationary (item A) rather than reduce unemployment (item D). The higher demand would also be satisfied to some extent by higher imports (Item C) and there would be supply bottlenecks caused by domestic firms being unable to meet the larger volume of orders for their output (item B).
24	D	Cost-push inflation is inflation caused by higher unit costs of production being passed through into higher prices. If wage increases are linked to productivity improvements (measure 2), labour costs of production will be kept down. A revaluation of the currency (measure 4) will make imported goods and raw materials cheaper to buy. Higher direct taxation (eg higher income tax) and higher interest rates would be intended to dampen **demand** in the economy, and would be measures for dealing with demand-pull inflation.
25	A	Diminishing returns occur when the marginal physical product of extra units of labour starts to decline. This begins to happen at output W, when the rate of increase in total output starts to decline as numbers employed continue to increase.

26	A	Item B is an external cost of the project, since increased volumes of traffic are harmful to the environment. Item C is a private benefit for the firm. Item D would only be an external benefit if a building is better for society than the use of open land, which is unlikely. Item A is correct because the benefits to local shops are additional to the private benefits of the sports firm and as such are external benefits.
27	D	This is because comparative advantage is measured in opportunity cost terms, not absolute cost terms.
28	B	Clearly, higher tariffs will drive up import prices and thus reduce the volume bought and sold.
29	B	A, C and D are the transactions, precautionary and speculative motives respectively.
30	A	Financial capital can be transferred electronically, as, to some extent, can technical knowledge. Technological workers and managers both have skills that are internationally applicable and the money to pay for travel.
31	C	The balance of payments current account deals with imports and exports, so A and B are wrong and D is irrelevant.
32	D	The improvement is dependent on a rise in exports and a fall in imports in response to price changes. Demand for both must be reasonably elastic if this is to occur. This is the basis of the Marshall-Learner condition.
33	C	A single interest rate is set for the whole euro bloc. Inevitably, some joiners will have existing rates that are greater than this, and some will have lower rates.
34	B	Export prices will only change if the rate changes. Exchange dealing costs remain the same. There is far more to international competitiveness than the exchange rate. Also, a floating exchange rate is affected by factors other than trade performance; these include the interest rate in particular.
35	C	The interest rate is the opportunity cost.
36	B	This will make sterling less attractive to hold.
37	D	The production possibility frontier (or curve) shows the maximum an economy can produce if it uses its limited resources efficiently. Unemployment represents an inefficiency in the labour market; such that current production falls short of the frontier. So a reduction in unemployment will bring actual production closer to the frontier, but will not expand it (to the right).
38	C	The increase in government spending will lead to an increased budget deficit.
39	B	Demand is inelastic (<1). Therefore an increase in price generates a less than proportional fall in demand such that total expenditure on the good rises.
40	A	The equilibrium price falls from A to C.
41	A	This is the profit maximization rule applicable to both price takers and price searchers.
42	C	While accounting profit and economic profit are both calculated by subtracting costs from revenues, the definition of total cost differs. Economic total cost includes implicit costs, whereas accounting total cost excludes the implicit cost of equity capital. An implicit cost is the opportunity cost for use of resources owned by the company.

43   D   They are automatic features that do not require a change in fiscal policy; for example tax revenues that rise as national income rises are an automatic stabiliser.

44   B   % change in quantity $= \dfrac{9,500 - 10,000}{(10,000 + 9,500) \div 2} = \dfrac{-500}{9,750} = -5.1\%$

             % change in price $= \dfrac{11 - 10}{(10 + 11) \div 2} = \dfrac{1}{10.5} = 9.5\%$

             Elasticity $= \dfrac{-5.1\%}{9.5\%} = -0.54$

45   B   The US dollar has appreciated, therefore the yen has depreciated and Japanese goods will be cheaper in the USA.

46   C   If fixed cost are zero, the total costs will by definition equal variable costs.

47   C   There is no one plant size that can produce at all points on the long run average total cost curve.

48   A   This is when a rise in government spending or a cut in tax rates leads to an increase in aggregate demand.

49   D   This reduces the level of excess reserves that banks hold.
           A lower level of excess reserves enhances the impact of the multiplier.

50   C   The US will specialize in the production of CD players while Germany will specialize in television production due to the relative production costs of each (comparative advantage).

51   B   Increased government spending causes increases in government borrowing, increasing interest rates and reducing private investment and government demand.

52   C   The currency that has the lower interest rates will be at a premium in the forward market.

53   A   The original Phillips curve indicated that there is an inverse relationship between the rate of inflation and the level of unemployment.

54   C   PED = 1 at $80, therefore any price movement will lead to a decrease in a firm's revenue. If P rises, we move onto the elastic part of the demand curve in which case the quantity demanded will fall by a greater percentage than the percentage increase in price. Conversely, if P falls, we move onto the inelastic part of the demand curve, in which case the quantity demanded will rise but by a smaller percentage than the fall in P.

55   A   A change in the price of the resource will cause a movement along the demand curve for the resource.

56   B

	Cashflow	Discount factor	
	$m	$m	$m
Investment			(10.0)
Year 1	3	× 0.909	2.73
Year 2	4	× 0.826	3.30
Year 3	5	× 0.751	3.76
			(0.21)

57	B	Bond prices are likely to move inventory with interest rates.
58	C	This may force firms to compete.
59	A	The firm will produce at the point where MC = MR.

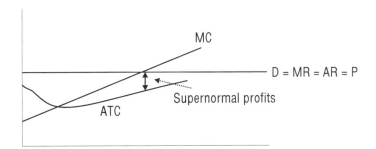

60	A	Bond prices are likely to move inversely with interest rates.
61	A	0.95 + 0.02. The bank will give less euro per $1 rather than more (ie 0.97 rather than 1.00).
62	A	When demand is inelastic, the quantity demanded is not very sensitive to price changes. Price and demand will move in the same direction but the increase will generally not be proportional.
63	B	Calculate the prices of US items in pounds and of British items in dollars, under the assumption that $1 = GB £5

Items	United States $	Dollar Price of British Items	British £	£ Price of US Items
Shoes	20	16	80	100
Watches	40	36	180	200
Electric motors	80	120	600	400

The United States gains by importing shoes and watches, and Britain gains by importing electric motors.

64	D	The Japanese automobile manufacturer will be buying dollars and selling yen.
65	A	An unexpected shift to a more expansionary monetary policy causes interest rates to fall.
66	C	The forward rate is a mathematical result of the difference in interest rates in the two countries.
67	C	Inflation-indexed bonds are issued with a fixed coupon. However, since the principal is adjusted to reflect inflation, so that dollar amount of the coupon will change with inflation.
68	C	$1.6 \times \dfrac{1.015}{1.02}$ = 1.5922. Remember to convert the interest rate to a three-monthly period by dividing by four.
69	C	Equity prices will normally fall.
70	A	The exchange rate will normally fall.

71   D   20%. $\dfrac{2.00}{0.08}$ = \$25; $\dfrac{2.00}{0.1}$ = \$20

$$\dfrac{25-20}{25} \times 100\% = 20\%$$

72   D   The 3 E's are economy, effectiveness and efficiency

73   B   Private investment

74   D   The tendency for balance of payments deficits to deepen before improving following a fall in the exchange rate.

75   A   Inelastic supply.

CIMA
Paper C4 (Certificate)
Fundamentals of Business Economics

Mock Assessment 2

Question Paper	
Time allowed	**2 hours**
Answer ALL seventy-five questions	

DO NOT OPEN THIS PAPER UNTIL YOU ARE READY TO START UNDER EXAMINATION CONDITIONS

Answer ALL questions

1   The 'central economic problem' is:

   A   The persistence of unemployment.
   B   The need to allocate scarce resources between competing uses.
   C   Consumers having less money than they would like.
   D   The need to ensure that in the long run all production costs are covered by sales revenue

2   Which *one* of the following would shift a country's production possibility frontier (PPF) *outwards* (away from the origin)?

   A   A fall in unemployment
   B   An increase in exports
   C   A rise in total consumer expenditure
   D   Technical progress reducing production costs

3   The term 'rising economic welfare' means:

   A   An increase in state welfare payments.
   B   A rising standard of living.
   C   Increased employment opportunities.
   D   Increased consumption of health and education services.

4   If an economy experiences an 'increase in productivity', this must mean that:

   A   The level of total output in the economy has risen.
   B   Employees are working harder than before.
   C   Output per unit of input has risen.
   D   Technical change has taken place.

5   Which *one* of the following is *not* an example of an external social cost?

   A   Reduction of oil reserves owing to increased use of cars
   B   River pollution caused by a manufacturing process
   C   Health problems caused by vehicle emissions
   D   Discarded packaging outside fast-food outlets

6   All of the following government policies would tend to raise the long-term rate of economic growth *except* which *one*?

   A   Encouraging a higher level of business investment
   B   Increasing expenditure on education and training
   C   Encouraging a higher level of consumer expenditure
   D   Providing tax relief for research and development expenditure by businesses

7   Which *one* of the following is most characteristic of a market economy?

A   Prices are determined mainly by market forces
B   Resources are allocated between different markets by administrative decisions
C   Consumer preferences are determined by market research
D   All markets are characterised by a high degree of competition

8   The demand curve for the product of a business will shift to the right when there is:

A   A reduction in indirect tax on the good
B   An improvement in production which lowers costs
C   A fall in the price of the good
D   An increase in the supply of a complementary good

9   If the demand for a firm's product has a price elasticity of −2, a 10 per cent *fall* in its price will:

A   Decrease total revenue by 20 per cent
B   Increase sales volume by 10 per cent
C   Increase sales volume by 20 per cent
D   Increase total revenue by 20 per cent

10   The short-run average-cost curve for firms rises after a certain level of output because of:

A   Diseconomies of scale
B   The law of diminishing returns
C   Diminishing marginal utility
D   Rising price of factors of production

11   The imposition of a minimum wage will cause unemployment in a labour market only if:

A   The demand for labour is elastic
B   The demand for labour is inelastic
C   The minimum wage is above the equilibrium wage
D   The minimum wage is below the equilibrium wage

12   Government may be concerned about the growth of monopoly power in an industry because monopolies:

A   Attempt to maximise profits
B   Restrict output
C   May secure economies of scale
D   Control a large share of the market

13   Which *one* of the following will tend to *increase* the degree of competition in an industry?

A   Product differentiation
B   Horizontal integration
C   Economies of scale
D   Low fixed costs

BPP
LEARNING MEDIA

28 The importance of saving in promoting economic growth is because of its relationship with:

A   Present consumption
B   Future consumption
C   Investment
D   Interest rates

29 Economic growth is desirable because it makes all of the following possible *except* which *one*?

A   The elimination of the economic problem
B   Higher living standards
C   Increased private and public consumption
D   Increased leisure

30 All of the following policies could promote export-led economic growth *except* which *one*?

A   A reduction in the country's tariffs on imports
B   A restrictive domestic monetary policy
C   The removal of taxes on employing labour
D   An appreciation in the country's foreign exchange rate

31 The cross elasticity of demand between Good A and Good B is +0.8%.

Which of the following must be true?

A   Goods A and B are complements
B   Goods A and B are substitutes
C   Good A is a luxury good
D   Good B is a Giffen good

32 Economies of scale are best described as the process by which

A   Large, dominant firms can secure higher profits
B   Large firms can better organise their factors of production
C   Large-scale production permits the use of new technology
D   Large-scale production leads to lower costs per unit of output

33 Which one of the following will tend to make the demand for a company's product less price elastic?

A   A change in fashion making the item more attractive
B   A rise in the price of complementary goods
C   A fall in the number of substitute goods
D   A lower price for the good

34   Which one of the following does *not* restrict the number of firms in an industry?

    A   Low levels of product differentiation
    B   Significant economies of scale
    C   Barriers to entry
    D   The use of capital-intensive technology in the industry

35   An airline sells standby passenger tickets at a much lower price than tickets bought in advance. This is because:

    A   Marginal cost is low for a seat up to the point where an aeroplane is fully occupied
    B   The average cost of a standby seat is lower than its marginal cost
    C   Selling additional tickets in this way will raise average revenue
    D   The demand for seats is always price-inelastic

36   The real rate of interest:

    A   Is the rate charged on loans
    B   Is the yield on irredeemable government stocks
    C   Equals the nominal interest rate adjusted for the rate of inflation
    D   Is the rate most relevant in making lending decisions

37   Which ONE of the following is an example of a non-tariff barrier?

    A   Price differences caused by import duties
    B   Differences in regulations between countries which prevent free trade
    C   Import duties
    D   Reductions in domestic production resulting from increased imports from low-cost countries

38   Which of the following costs should a firm's revenue cover for the firm to continue production in the short run?

    A   Total costs
    B   Total variable costs
    C   Total fixed costs
    D   Average total costs

39   Which of the following are true?

    (i)   A straight line demand curve displays constant elasticity at all points along its length.
    (ii)   A supply curve with unit elasticity is a straight line along all its length

    A   Neither
    B   (i) only
    C   (ii) only
    D   Both

40 A supply curve will shift to the right if there is a rise in the price of other goods.

☐ True
☐ False

41 If the US is a low opportunity cost producer of wine and there are free international trade markets

A The US will export wine and the US price for wine will be higher than in a market with no international trade

B The US will export wine and the US price for wine will be lower than in a market with no international trade

C The US will not export wine, giving a higher price for wine in the US than the price elsewhere in the world

D The US will not export wine, giving a lower price for wine in the US than the price elsewhere in the world

42 In macroeconomics, the crowding-out effect refers to

A The impact of government deficit spending on inflation
B A situation in which the unemployment rate is below its natural rate
C The impact of government borrowing on interest rates and private investment
D Increasing population pressures and associated movements toward zero population growth

43 The public in a country decides to decrease its holdings of currency and to increase its holdings of checking account funds by an equal amount. If the country's central bank does not take any offsetting actions, how will the money supply be affected?

A The money supply will decrease

B The money supply will not be affected because the increase in checking account holdings will offset the decrease in currency holdings

C The action does not directly affect the money supply, but the action will reduce the excess reserves of banks and tend to reduce the money supply indirectly

D The action does not directly affect the money supply, but the action will increase the excess reserves of banks and tend to increase the money supply because banks may expand their loans

44 A 10 percent increase in income caused a group of consumers to increase their purchases of television sets by 10%. What would be the group's income elasticity of demand for television sets?

A 0.10
B 0.20
C 1.00
D 2.00

45   How would an unanticipated shift to a more expansionary monetary policy in the United States typically affect the short term demand for foreign currencies in the United States and the value of the US dollar?

	Demand for Foreign Currencies	Foreign Exchange Value of the Dollar
A	Increase	No change
B	Increase	Decrease
C	No change	Decrease
D	Decrease	Increase

46   Which one of the following statements *least likely* reflects the law of comparative advantage?

A   Specialisation and exchange will permit trading partners to maximize their joint output

B   A nation cannot gain from trade when its trading partners are low-wage countries

C   A nation can gain from trade even when it has an absolute disadvantage in the production of all goods

D   A nation will import goods in which it has the highest opportunity cost of production

47   Which of the following is not a component in the calculation of the balance of payments for a particular country?

A   Net investment income
B   Transfers of funds
C   Private capital flows
D   Net domestic loans

48   Which of the following statements regarding a shallow straight-line demand curve is *most accurate*?

A   It will exhibit price inelasticity only
B   It will exhibit price elasticity only
C   It will exhibit price elasticity and price inelasticity only
D   It will exhibit price elasticity, price inelasticity and price unitary elasticity

49   Which one of the following statements regarding a monopolist is *most accurate*?

A monopolist:

A   Faces a horizontal demand curve
B   Will produce at the minimum of average total cost
C   Is normally assumed to be a sales revenue maximiser
D   Will produce where marginal revenue equals marginal cost

50 Which of the following is/are true in respect of price discrimination?

   (i) It may result in the production of more goods
   (ii) It is confined to monopoly markets

	Statement (i)	Statement (ii)
A	True	False
B	False	True
C	True	True
D	False	False

51 Which of the following are a result of high entry barriers?

   A Increased price competition
   B More efficient utilisation of resources
   C An increase in consumer choice
   D Allocative inefficiency

52 Which one of the following statements regarding Purchasing Power Parity theory (PPP) is correct?

   A PPP predicts that the country with the higher inflation rate will have a strengthening currency

   B PPP predicts that the country with a higher interest rate will have a strengthening currency

   C PPP predicts that the country with the higher inflation rate will have a weakening currency

   D An implication of PPP is that only nominal exchange rates are of significance

53 Where multiple measures are employed, a rational producer will utilise a resource until

   A The marginal product per last dollar spent is the same for all resources used
   B The marginal revenue product is the same for all resources used
   C The price is the same for all resources used
   D The cost is the same for all resources used

54 Which of the following is the best description of the substitution effect? and income

   A The substitution effect is part of the reason that the demand curve is downward sloping. It explains the movement to a new indifference curve

   B The substitution effect is part of the reason that the demand curve is downward sloping. It explains the movement along the original indifference curve

   C The substitution effect is part of the reason that the supply curve is upward sloping. It explains the movement along the original indifference curve

   D The substitution effect is part of the reason that the supply curve is upward sloping. It explains the movement along the original indifference curve

MOCK ASSESSMENT 2: QUESTIONS

55   Which of the following is least likely to be an automatic stabiliser?

    A   Progressive income taxes
    B   Unemployment compensation benefits
    C   Import tariffs
    D   Corporate taxation

56   Which of the following controls the level of interest rates?

    A   Commercial banks
    B   The reserve asset ratio
    C   The capital markets
    D   The central bank

57   The reserve requirement is 10% and the Central Bank sells 20m of government bonds. What will the impact of this be on money supply?

    A   Increase by 200m
    B   Decrease by 200m
    C   Increase by 2m
    D   Decrease by 2m

58   A monopolist will produce a quantity of goods such that

    A   Marginal revenue is zero
    B   Marginal cost is minimised
    C   Marginal revenue equals marginal cost
    D   Average revenue equals marginal cost

59   The law of comparative advantage will hold so long as a country has what advantage in producing a good?

    A   Relative advantage
    B   Recurring advantage
    C   Absolute advantage
    D   Real advantage

60   Which of the following would enable a country to reduce its levels of imports in a fixed exchange rate regime?

    A   Selling foreign currency reserves
    B   Increasing the budget deficit
    C   Imposing quotas
    D   Imposing controls on overseas investment

61 Which of the following is a valid conclusion if the exchange rate of the British pound against the US dollar changes from $1.90 to $1.70?

A   The pound has appreciated, and the British pay more for US goods
B   The pound has depreciated, and the British pay more for US goods
C   The pound has appreciated, and the British pay less for US goods
D   The pound has depreciated, and the British pay less for US goods

62 Which of the following would occur if, under a flexible system of exchange rates, the US were to impose a tariff on major imported items?

A   Increase the balance of trade deficit of the US
B   Cause the dollar to depreciate in value
C   Increase the balance of payments deficit of the US
D   Cause the dollar to appreciate in value

63 Given a flexible exchange rate system, which of the following is more likely to cause a country's currency to appreciate on the foreign exchange market?

A   Stable prices at home, but trading partners having inflation
B   An unanticipated increase in the money supply
C   Decreases in domestic interest rates
D   Inflation at home, but trading partners having stable prices

64 Under a flexible exchange rate system, a nation that offers more attractive investment opportunities than its trading partners could experience a

A   Current account surplus
B   Current account deficit
C   Financial account deficit
D   Balance of trade surplus

65 Which of the following would an economist use to describe a situation where Nation A can produce a product with fewer resources than Nation B?

A   Nation A has a comparative advantage in production of the product
B   Nation A incurs a higher opportunity cost in producing the product
C   Nation A should be a net importer of the product
D   Nation A has an absolute advantage in production of the product

66 Which of the following accurately describes the short-term and long-term economic impact of import quotas on the creation of jobs?

A   Import quotas increase jobs in both the short run and long run
B   Import quotas have no impact in the short run, but increase jobs in the long run
C   Import quotas increase jobs in the short run, but not in the long run
D   Import quotas have no impact on jobs in the short run or long run

67 Which of the following would most likely occur if aggregate demand exceeds the economy's long run capacity?

A   Increases in real output, aggregate supply, and total capacity
B   A decrease in the interest rate
C   Inflation (increase in price levels)
D   Increase in unemployment, causing the economy's aggregate supply to shift to the right

68 Monopolistic competition is indicated by which of the following descriptions?

A   A single seller with high barriers to entry
B   A small number of sellers with high barriers to entry
C   A large number of sellers with complete freedom of entry and exit
D   A large number of sellers with low barriers to entry

69 Which of the following is the primary determinant of price elasticity of demand?

A   Consumer choice and income
B   Whether complementary goods can be found
C   Whether substitutes for the good are available
D   Producer inventory levels

70 The relationship between risk and return is a positive one because

A   Investors require a compensation for investing in risky assets
B   The yield curve is also positively sloped
C   Investors love risk
D   Investors prefer liquid assets

71 A good coffee harvest (due to good weather) leads to a lower price of coffee. This happens because

A   The coffee supply curve shifted to the right
B   The coffee supply curve shifted to the left
C   Both the coffee supply and demand curves shifted to the right
D   The coffee demand curve shifted down

72 A good with a vertical demand curve implies that a change (shift) in supply

A   Will not affect the equilibrium price
B   Will not affect the equilibrium quantity
C   Will not affect the equilibrium price and the quantity
D   Will create a surplus or a shortage

73 A firm in a perfectly competitive industry that maximises its profits in the long run

A   Selects a level of output that minimises total cost
B   Selects the level of output at which marginal cost equals the price
C   Select the level of output that minimises marginal cost
D   Selects the level of output that minimises variable costs

74   A vertical supply curve

    A   Has slope equal to zero

    B   Has an own price elasticity equal to 0

    C   Has an own price elasticity equal to infinity

    D   Has own price elasticity equal to 1

75   A country will increase its foreign currency reserves if:

    A   There is a favourable balance of trade with intervention in currency markets

    B   There is a favourable balance of trade and the government intervenes to hold its currency down

    C   It devalues the currency

    D   It runs a trade deficit

Answers

DO NOT TURN THIS PAGE UNTIL YOU HAVE
COMPLETED MOCK ASSESSMENT 2

1	B	The allocation of scarce resources is the essence of economics.
2	D	A fall in unemployment would move output towards the PPF from within. An increase in exports is merely a change in the pattern of consumption. A rise in consumer spending would lead to inflation if output was already on the PPF.
3	B	Economic welfare is about consumption of all kinds (except demerit goods).
4	C	A could happen without a productivity increase; for example, more resources might become available. B would be one way productivity could rise, but is not the only way. Similarly, productivity increases (D) can follow from technical improvements, but this is not the only source.
5	A	Depletion of oil reserves is a consequence internal to the sale of oil; the other items are external to the economic transactions that bring them about, that is, they affect people who are not parties to the transactions.
6	C	A, B and D will affect supply and move the PPF outwards. C is a demand measure and can only help if the economy is under-performing. If the economy is producing at its maximum potential, increasing demand alone will lead to inflation rather than growth.
7	A	B is typical of a planned economy. D is not a state of affairs that can realistically be expected – the existence of natural monopolies alone would ensure that. C describes an attempt to anticipate market forces.
8	D	A and B will affect supply, C will change the quantity demanded by a move along the demand curve.
9	C	A and D are incorrect because elasticity is by definition about **quantity demanded**. B is arithmetically incorrect.
10	B	A is a long run effect. C determines the shape of the demand curve. D is wrong because the theory of short run costs assumes stable prices.
11	C	D is simply wrong. B is plausible, but the demand curve would have to be vertical, that is **perfectly** inelastic, which is not a real world condition at all.
12	B	A, C and D can be true of many firms that do not approach monopoly power. B is true but to some extent incomplete: monopolies restrict output to maximise their profit and this has undesirable consequences such as higher prices than under perfect competition and lower allocative efficiency.
13	D	A and C form barriers to entry. B reduces the number of firms trading in the market. D makes entry into the market and exit from it easy.
14	C	Money can be used to acquire factors of production but is not itself a factor.
15	A	B is a separate characteristic typical of oligopolies. C is not always true where collusion is illegal; even where firms do not collude they must consider their competitors' reactions to any change in their own pricing policy. D is not entirely true: reactions to price changes are largely predictable, though not in detail.
16	C	B adjusts total domestic expenditure to GDP at market prices and A converts GDP at **market price** to GDP at **factor cost**, when using the expenditure approach. Trading in second hand goods is a value-adding service.

17	B	Higher interest rates make borrowing to invest more expensive.
18	D	Tax revenues increase and welfare payments decrease during the upswing, so a higher proportion of government spending can be funded from tax.
19	C	Inflation will cause money value revenue to rise; revenue in real terms will not change. Expansion of the money supply may lead to inflation rather than vice versa. Inflation reduces the real value of both financial assets and the income they produce.
20	A	B is demand deficient unemployment, as is D. Inflation is usually associated with excess demand and therefore with rising employment.
21	B	A would not really affect supply or demand. C is actually an increase in demand for a particular type of good. D would tend to prevent improvements in supply by protecting the *status quo*.
22	D	Capital account is concerned with investment flows. A, B and C are all current account items.
23	C	This is impossible with a single currency.
24	C	They would remain the same in domestic currency.
25	B	Globalisation generates an increased *interdependence* of national economies, which is the opposite of option B.
26	B	An attempt is made to charge for a public good.
27	D	This is a definition.
28	C	Present consumption is reduced by saving: this reduction in demand can have a negative effect on growth as in Japan 1990-2002. Saving can provide for future consumption but the extent to which consumption increases in the future will promote growth is debatable. High levels of saving *may* exert some downward pressure on interest rates or, at least, modify an upward pressure, but this effect is likely to be very small.
29	A	People's wants will never be satisfied and hence the economic problem will never be eliminated.
30	D	This would make exports more expensive to buy. A might encourage reciprocal treatment by other countries. B would reduce domestic demand, making more goods available for export. C would reduce the cost and hence, possibly, the price of exports.
31	B	Cross elasticity of demand is positive for substitutes and negative for complements.
32	D	This is a definition, almost.
33	C	D will simply demonstrate the elasticity that is present. A and B may shift the demand curve but are unlikely to affect its elasticity. Availability of substitutes is a key influence on price elasticity of demand.
34	A	Scale economies and the need for heavy investment are themselves barriers to entry, since they demand major capital resources to overcome. The lower the degree of differentiation, the closer the approach is to perfect competition.
35	A	The plane will fly anyway: carrying an extra passenger costs relatively little.
36	C	The real rate of interest is the amount by which nominal rates exceed inflation.

37	B	Sometimes, excessive 'red tape' regulations might be deliberately imposed as a means of protection.
38	B	A firm will have to pay fixed costs in the short run regardless of whether it continues production. Therefore it is beneficial to carry on producing, provided that the variable costs incurred in production are covered.
39	C	A supply curve with unit elasticity is a straight line, but note that a demand curve with unit elasticity is *not* a straight line. A straight line demand curve is elastic for low quantities of demand, and gets progressively less elastic as quantity increases.
40	False.	The production of the good will be less attractive if the price of other goods rises. Less will be offered at any price.
41	A	This is because the world price of wine is likely to be higher than the equilibrium price in the US without trade.
42	C	Government spending financed by borrowing will drive up interest rates reducing the amount of borrowing possible by the private sector. As a result, private investment will fall.
43	D	Excess reserves is defined as the excess of actual reserves over required reserves.
44	C	Income elasticity of demand equals percentage change in quantity demanded divided by the percentage change in income 10%/10% = 1.00
45	B	An expansionary monetary policy will cause growth in domestic income, higher prices and increased imports. This will therefore lead to an increased demand for foreign currency and a weaker US dollar.
46	B	There will always be scope for gains from specialisation so long as there is some variation in the relative opportunity cost of goods.

47   D   The components in any balance of payments calculation are

(i) balance of merchandise trade
(ii) balance of goods and services   } current account
(iii) net investment income
(iv) net transfers
(v) private capital flows   } financial account

48	D	Most demand curves exhibit the full range of elasticities.
49	D	Only in perfect competition is output at the minimum average total cost (B). Firms are assumed to be profit maximisers rather than sales revenue maximisers (C).
50	A	Price discrimination is only not possible in a perfectly competitive industry.
51	D	When the price charged does not equal the marginal cost of production, there is allocative inefficiency. Allocative efficiency is only achieved under perfect competition, where there are no barriers to entry.
52	C	PPP is concerned with relative prices (inflation) and not interest rates. If the rate of inflation is higher in one country than another, the value of its currency will tend to weaken against the other country's currency.

53   A   For example,

$$\frac{Marginal\ product_{skilled\ labour}}{Price_{skilled\ labour}} = \frac{Marginal\ product_{unskilled\ labour}}{Price_{unskilled\ labour}} = \frac{Marginal\ product_{machinery}}{Price_{machinery}}$$

54   B   The other effect that explains the downward sloping demand curve is the income effect.

55   C   Import tariffs do not automatically vary with the economic cycle.

56   D   The central bank.

57   B $20m \times \dfrac{1}{0.1}$ will be taken out of the money supply.

(handwritten: $100 - 10$ × $-20M$. $20 \cdot \dfrac{10}{10} = 200$)

58   C   This is the profit maximising condition common to **all** theories of the firm.

59   A   Even though it may have an absolute advantage in a number of products.

60   C   A would only lead to a strengthening of the currency. B would boost demand, hence imports.

61   B   Because one pound now exchanges for fewer dollars, the pound has depreciated in value against the dollar. The British will find the price of dollar denominated goods higher as more of their currency will be required to purchase US goods.

62   D   Domestic consumers will demand less of the import (reducing the trade deficit), and a corresponding decrease will occur in demand for the applicable foreign currency. The foreign currency will depreciate relative to the dollar, if the foreign currency has depreciated relative to the dollar, than the dollar has appreciated relative to the foreign currency.

63   A   Stable domestic prices allow foreign customers to pay the same amount for goods while inflation abroad will likely cause higher prices for foreign goods. Foreign customers increase demand for the less expensive domestic goods and cause the domestic currency to appreciate in value on the foreign exchange market.

64   B   The attractive investment opportunities could create demand for the currency, causing the currency to appreciate. This will cause exports to fall, creating a current account deficit.

65   D   Nation A is said to hold an absolute advantage in the production of a good when it can produce more of the good, using the same amount of resources (or the same amount of goods using fewer resources) than another country. Nation A's opportunity cost for producing the product would be lower than Nation B's, and would not provide incentive for them to import the product. Comparative advantage occurs between trading partners that specialise in production of certain goods, and exchange for others, such that both partners maximize their output. We cannot tell whether Nation A has a comparative advantage without further information.

66   C   Quotas are designed to protect domestic industry by restricting the import of competing foreign goods. Quotas increase jobs in the protected industry in the short run. However, decreasing demand for foreign products decreases foreign access to the domestic currency necessary to purchase domestic exports. The long-term effect is a reduction in jobs in unprotected export industries due to a decreased demand for domestic exports.

67   C   Increases in real GDP beyond an economy's long run capacity are temporary. They last until fixed resource prices adjust and cause inflation.

68   D   Monopolistic competition is a misleading term often used by economists to describe a large number of sellers supplying differentiated products to a market with low barriers to entry. A more descriptive and less misleading term for such markets is competitive price-searcher market.

                A single seller of a differentiated product with high barrier to entry would be considered a monopoly. Additional sellers of a differentiated product, but with high barriers to entry describes an oligopoly. A perfectly competitive market (also known as a price-taker market) has a large number of sellers with complete freedom of entry and exit.

69   C   Price elasticity of demand is determined by the availability of substitutes. When substitutes for a product can be purchased, price increases cause consumers to switch to other products. If substitutes cannot be found, demand for the product will be inelastic.

70   A   The relationship is positive because investors require a higher return to compensate for investing in riskier assets.

71   A   The coffee supply curve shifted to the right.

72   B   Will not affect the equilibrium quantity because there is only one level of demand (hence the vertical demand curve).

73   B   Selects the level of output at which marginal cost equals the price

74   B   Has an own price elasticity of 0 (perfectly inelastic supply). A vertical supply curve indicates supply does not change despite a change in price.

75   B   There is a favourable balance of trade and the government intervenes to hold the currency down.

Review Form & Free Prize Draw – Paper C4 Fundamentals of Business Economics (12/07)

All original review forms from the entire BPP range, completed with genuine comments, will be entered into one of two draws on 31 July 2008 and 31 January 2009. The names on the first four forms picked out on each occasion will be sent a cheque for £50.

Name: _____ **Address:** _____

_____

_____

How have you used this Kit?
(Tick one box only)

☐ Home study (book only)

☐ On a course: college _____

☐ With 'correspondence' package

☐ Other _____

Why did you decide to purchase this Kit?
(Tick one box only)

☐ Have used the complementary Study text

☐ Have used other BPP products in the past

☐ Recommendation by friend/colleague

☐ Recommendation by a lecturer at college

☐ Saw advertising

☐ Other _____

During the past six months do you recall seeing/receiving any of the following?
(Tick as many boxes as are relevant)

☐ Our advertisement in *CIMA Insider*

☐ Our advertisement in *Financial Management*

☐ Our advertisement in *Pass*

☐ Our brochure with a letter through the post

☐ Our website www.bpp.com

Which (if any) aspects of our advertising do you find useful?
(Tick as many boxes as are relevant)

☐ Prices and publication dates of new editions

☐ Information on product content

☐ Facility to order books off-the-page

☐ None of the above

Which BPP products have you used?

Text	☐	Kit	☑	i-Pass	☐
Passcard	☐	CD	☐		
Big Picture Poster	☐	Virtual Campus	☐		

Your ratings, comments and suggestions would be appreciated on the following areas.

	Very useful	Useful	Not useful
Effective revision	☐	☐	☐
Exam guidance	☐	☐	☐
Multiple choice questions	☐	☐	☐
Objective test questions	☐	☐	☐
Guidance in answers	☐	☐	☐
Content and structure of answers	☐	☐	☐
Mock assessments	☐	☐	☐
Mock assessment answers	☐	☐	☐

Overall opinion of this Kit   Excellent ☐   Good ☐   Adequate ☐   Poor ☐

Do you intend to continue using BPP products?   Yes ☐   No ☐

The BPP author of this edition can be e-mailed at: adrianthomas@bpp.com

Please return this form to: Janice Ross, CIMA Certificate Publishing Manager, BPP Learning Media Ltd, FREEPOST, London, W12 8BR

Review Form & Free Prize Draw (continued)

TELL US WHAT YOU THINK

Please note any further comments and suggestions/errors below

Free Prize Draw Rules

1 Closing date for 31 July 2008 draw is 30 June 2008. Closing date for 31 January 2009 draw is 31 December 2008.

2 Restricted to entries with UK and Eire addresses only. BPP employees, their families and business associates are excluded.

3 No purchase necessary. Entry forms are available upon request from BPP Learning Media Ltd. No more than one entry per title, per person. Draw restricted to persons aged 16 and over.

4 Winners will be notified by post and receive their cheques not later than 6 weeks after the relevant draw date.

5 The decision of the promoter in all matters is final and binding. No correspondence will be entered into.

Central Bank increasing money supply $\Rightarrow$ ↓ decreasing discount rate $\Rightarrow$

$\Rightarrow$ reducing the level of excess reserves that bank holds

$\Rightarrow$ lower level of excess reserve $\Rightarrow$ enhance the impact of MULTIPLIER

Forward exchange rate $\rightarrow$ ↓ interest rate currency will be at premium.

upswing phase trade cycle ; ↓ unemployment
↑ level of imports
↑ National Income
↓ Gov. Borrowing

↑ Tax revenues
↓ welfare payments

import goods $\rightarrow$ ↑ opportunity cost
export good $\rightarrow$ ↓ low opportunity cost

Tax border Buyer/Consumer
D- Inelastic
S- Elastic
Tax border minimize
D-Inel.
S-Inelastic